THE CLASSIC YEARS
OF
ROBERT A. HEINLEIN

MORE WILDSIDE CLASSICS

Please see www.wildsidepress.com for a complete list!

THE CLASSIC YEARS OF ROBERT A. HEINLEIN

by

GEORGE EDGAR SLUSSER

WILDSIODE PRESS

To Mike and Mary

THE CLASSIC YEARS OF ROBERT A. HEINLEIN

This edition published in 2006 by Wildside Press, LLC.
www.wildsidepress.com

THE CLASSIC YEARS

No sooner is the title set down than it must be put to the question: what is a "classic" Heinlein work? Most criticism of Heinlein begins and ends here. Invariably, each individual critic has chosen the works he likes best, dubbed them classics, and consigned the rest to oblivion. But if the question can be pegged, the term can also be abandoned. Before doing so, however, I wish to discuss its implicatons and former applications. What better way to discuss the problems of Heinlein's fiction? The years to be covered in this study include, basically, the 1940s and 1950s—the period of the stories and novellas, and the novels of juvenile adventure. Unfortunately, there is no touchstone which allows a reader infallibly to pick "classics" out of this span. What is possible, however, is a definition of process that will permit us to study Heinlein's evolution as a writer over two long and full decades.

It had been customary to divide Heinlein's vast production into "periods." Alexei Panshin, in his *Heinlein in Dimension*, gives three: the early years of "influence" (1929-1942); the middle years of "success" (1947-1958); and the later years of "alienation"(1959-date). Panshin's scheme is the old one of youth, maturity, and age. Obviously, the middle period is the "classic" one, dominated by novels of adventure which appear to strike a balance between convention and idiosyncrasy. Panshin's attitude toward the first period is only apparently laudatory. True, he sees Heinlein springing full-born into literary existence—by "influence," he means the revolutionary impact of this early fiction on SF in general. Yet the curiously episodic structure of these earliest stories perplexes him; and in specific critical judgments, he tends to treat them as apprentice work anyway. The third period is clearly one of failing powers. Increasing didacticism and belligerence overwhelm the story line, and the rambling monstrosities of this last, senescent period are born.

This schema is both inadequate and misleading. Panshin's descriptive tags refer to audience acceptance, not structural changes. Implicit here, however, are judgments in terms of the latter: because a work is unsuccessful, or because the fans don't like it, it must somehow be different, and therefore worse. The only structural norm appears to be the familiar and conventional. There is actually very little of this anywhere in Heinlein. In my earlier study, *Robert A. Heinlein: Stranger in His Own Land, Second Edition*, I consider Panshin's "alienation" as a matter of forms and their alteration: these late novels transform the conventions of the adventure narrative and direct them to new ends. I also show that this process of "alienation" begins well inside the "success" period: the problematical works of the 1960s are, in a very real sense, extensions of such subverted narratives as the "classic" novel, *Double Star*. This present essay would complicate matters even further, by demonstrating not only that "subversion" is actually an on-going process throughout this whole middle period. but that the structural oddities which so annoy the critic in Heinlein's later novels are already present in his earliest tales and novellas. In this sense, Heinlein was "alien" from the first story he wrote.

If Heinlein's development has three steps, then, to what extent are these successive and different—an ABC sequence? Or is the order actually ABA, in which the works of the end return to the beginning, if on a grander scale? The answer is perhaps a subtle combination of the two: the third period works are both similar to and different from those of the first, A and C. They result from the meeting of two contrary structural patterns. One is apparently basic to Heinlein's world view; it is present from the start. The other comes to him with the adventure conventions he adopts, built into the forms themselves through a long tradition of epic action in Western and American literature. Heinlein struggles with this pattern, but does not reject it so much as empty it, making it serve his basic ethos. The fundamental Heinlein, then, is to be found in the stories and novellas of period A. But the most interesting and dynamic Heinleins are the curious adventure novels and the B period.

Indeed, if chronological periods are marked off at all, they must be ordered in terms of genre. The use of a given form, in Heinlein's case, was dictated in large part during these early and middle years by the vagaries of science fiction publishing. His first (and only) market was pulp magazines, so he wrote short stories and novella-length serials. The switch to novels after the war (new publishing channels had opened up, and Panshin speculates Heinlein's motives were financial) demanded that he adopt the strict formulas and conventions imposed by his market—in this case, juvenile adventure. The middle period, then, begins with Heinlein's first full-length novel conceived as such, the space epic *Rocket Ship Galileo* (1947), and ends when what I call the subverted adventure finally rears its ugly head in *Starship Troopers* (1959)—in other words, from his first Scribner's juvenile to the first juvenile Scribner's rejected. Not all the novels of this period were juvenile, however. Two old serials were quickly published as novels: *Beyond the Horizon* (1948) and *Sixth Column* (1949). In 1951, Doubleday published Heinlein's first original "adult" novel, *The Puppet Masters*. The novels of this decade are basically of two sorts: the adolescent space adventure dominates—these are novels of initiation to manhood, in which a boy comes of age in outer space. The adult works are novels of political intrigue. But they also, in a sense, are stories of initiation. The heroes are young men instead of boys, and their field of action the "grown-up" world of nations and espionage. Still, they have as much to learn, and the situation is meant to test (and teach) them. In fact, these two modes tend to conflate in the later novels of the period. *Citizen of the Galaxy* (1957) has a boy hero who grows to be a young man; it has space adventure, political intrigue, and much more.

A fascination with politics and intrigue is constant throughout Heinlein's career, but spy novels, like those he wrote in the 1950s, are not. Many of the early stories are about behind-the-scenes manipulations, plotting, and scheming of one sort or another. Apparently, this same interest continues through the 1960s as well: a work like *The Moon is a Harsh Mistress* (1966), with its revolutionary setting and interplanetary intrigues, seems to carry on the tradition. This surface unity is deceptive, however. In Heinlein's early narratives, the focus is usually on the problem—the mechanics of plotting—not on the hero.

4

Only rarely is there concern with the formation of the individual in action. And what little there is remains minimal: these are not (to use Panshin's phrase) "people stories." In a work like *Moon*, similarly there is a shift away from personal action and growth. As with the subverted patterns of *Double Star*, here too the thrust of the intrigue is redirected to other, illustrative ends. But where the early stories dwell on external mechanics, *Moon* focuses on a more fundamental mechanism—the rhythms that link man and his destiny. Only in the middle novels does Heinlein even come close to the traditional cloak and dagger thriller. Only here is he concerned at all with the growth of an individual hero.

The juvenile pattern is more clearly circumscribed—it belongs essentially to the 1950s. At best, initiation is a perfunctory concern in Heinlein's early narratives. In a story like "Misfit," we have the barest outline of a juvenile: an unlikely boy exhibits an unsuspected talent for math; in a pinch, he takes the place of an ailing computer, and a delicate piece of space-jockeying is accomplished. In the later novels of boyish heroism, however, this process of self-discovery, the rites of passage, are far less static, much more arduous. Even the feats of the intellect, which Heinlein relishes, can be made infinitely more dynamic and suspenseful. Nor does the juvenile really survive the 1950s. A work like *Glory Road* is an anachronism, an oddly self-conscious version of a pattern that has been thoroughly transformed in *Stranger in a Strange Land* and the "philosophical" novels that follow it.

These conventional patterns of heroic adventure and formation dominate the works of the 1950s. And yet, as patterns they seem in many ways contrary to Heinlein's deep-seated vision of things. In contrast to the juvenile novels, few of his early narratives have tight construction, or even "plots" at all. Indeed the episodic, almost impressionistic nature of these works has always puzzled critics. They expect "character studies" in the traditional sense, where an individual shapes himself and is shaped in the matrix of free choice and chance event. They do not get them. On the contrary, Heinlein seems most willing to exploit the other, anecdotal tradition of the short story. In like manner, the tendency of serialized narratives to decompose into a row of autonomous units appears to favor rather than hinder his sense of construction. Behind the looseness of these forms, in fact, lies a much different basic pattern—call it predestination. In Heinlein's stories, man's acts do not carry through, nor do they link future sections in causal fashion, so much as illustrate, in any number of particular, exemplary moments, the workings of an immutable higher order.

In light of this, it is tempting to set aside the juvenile novels, and seek the germ of Heinlein's later problem fiction solely in these early stories and novellas. True, *Time Enough for Love* seems prefigured in the early *Beyond This Horizon* (serialized in 1941)—both as a narrative rooted in a "philosophical" quest (the hero, one of the "star-line," asks the question: why procreate?), and as a structure of multiple episodes (the center of what Panshin calls a "roman-candle plot" is the need, through cumulative experiences, to persuade

5

Hamilton Felix to do his part). In the same way, "Gulf" (1949) appears to bear the seed of a much vaster *Stranger in a Strange Land*. The middle novels, however, cannot be ignored as anomalies. On the contrary, they are the crucial step in Heinlein's development as a writer. There is no sudden conversion from formless episodic works to tightly wrought stories of adventure. A juvenile like *The Rolling Stones*, with its loose string of incidents, is proof that the old Heinlein abides. Nor are these adventure patterns simply abandoned, either. Heinlein retains them in his late novels, but has modified their form and function. Because of this, *Stranger* is both a different and far more complex literary experience than "Gulf." Now, the linear thrust of individual action has itself been suspended: it becomes but another episode in a much vaster exemplum. Like "Gulf," *Stranger* is an allegory of election—but one that subsumes the menace of the heroic deed, rather than ignoring it.

A pattern of election and predestination is dominant throughout Heinlein's work. It exists most visibly and openly in the early tales and novellas, and here it should first be grasped. Significantly, among these stories tight plots occur only in those that celebrate the workings of inexorable destiny—time-travel paradoxes, and various tales of sacrifice. In the latter, a man (he may be any size or shape, with results ranging from "tragic" to comic) is chosen, and simply accepts to do the job. He neither rebels against the machine, nor sets himself above it—he takes his place unhesitatingly in its workings.

The looser structures seem, contrarily, to center on the exploits of one powerful personality. If we look more closely, however, we see that he too, paradoxically, is more chosen than chooser. He achieves rank and power, but less through personal actions than by a special "vision," a predisposition. The most extraordinary of these is Delos D. Harriman, "the man who sold the moon." He appears as an entrepreneur of Balzacian proportions, able to organize and direct his army of specialists to fantastic doings that reach beyond governments and planetary boundaries. Yet this apotheosis of individuality, if we compare him with a Vautrin, is oddly transparent as an individual. His own emotional and spiritual struggles, as manifest in his actions, are not only banal but almost non-existent. In fact, we hardly see him act at all; most of his time is spent mapping plans. The texture of this novella is no more than a series of moot dialogues, which allow Harriman to unfold his fabulous scheme as he out-argues his opponents. Indeed, the most tenacious of these opponents are not individual men, but things and concepts—laws, institutions, natural barriers. Delos's insights open windows, laying bare various power structures. Instead of acting, he shows us how others act. Indeed, Harriman need only expose his plan, and miraculously it comes to pass—we know not how, or against what opposition, for all of this happens behind the scenes. Is a certain part of humanity predestined to go to the Moon? The narrator purposely does not give us the struggles and failures of this hero. Harriman's role is, instead, a revelatory one—he is the new Moses exposing the divine destiny of his chosen people.

In work after work, we observe secret societies within society emerging—it is their organization rather than their actions that interest Heinlein. These narratives are little more than elaborate rituals of sifting: in a given situation, the wheat is gradually separated from the chaff; we discover who is the true elite, who the false. Invariably, Heinlein's in-groups are formed of the most disparate and unlikely people: pot-bellied men, little old ladies, plain-looking joes who in reality are "supermen." As the true chain of power fuses and joins, official castes or hierarchies often break down. Their pseudo-leaders prove incompetent, unable to function—all along, their titles and honors were empty. Thus Harriman's chief engineer, Bob Coster, can tell the Vice President of the United States to "pipe down," and get away with it. In that supreme moment of truth which is Moonflight, the real elite emerges, the ornamental one fades away. Heinlein's elite are not known by physical signs, nor do they bear the traditional hero's stamp. Their deeds do not really designate them (they may give sample displays of power, no more). Instead, their true work is a common mental disposition: they believe in individual freedom, and are willing to band together to fight entangling bureaucracy and mass strictures. The goal of these libertarians is simply to keep the channels of election open: who can tell when or where another mute inglorious Milton may emerge? Significantly, once their own society within society is formed, they proceed to develop even tighter regulations than the structures they replace. What was custom on the outside takes on the force of code and ritual inside.

Critics have noticed Heinlein's *laissez faire* "philosophy," passing it off as primitive. What they have not noticed, however, is that this philosophy is rooted in much deeper soil, in patterns that are both cultural and mythical. The advent of religion in *Stranger* and the other later novels is no accident, nor is the harshly Calvinistic nature of this creed. Calvinistic figurations are present in Heinlein's earliest stories—they run throughout his work in one form or another. These variations, however, are important: there are three discernable phases. The first, essentially but not exclusively that of the early stories and novellas, could be called the Puritan phase—Heinlein's emphasis in these stories is on worldly hierarchies of the elect. At the point, in the juvenile novels, where predestination and conventional heroic patterns meet, we have a second, more "democratic" phase: the rule of the visionary company gives way momentarily to the possibility of Everyman as hero. The third phase, that of *Stranger* and its kindred novels, is more purely Calvinist. The mechanisms of election are reaffirmed; but, as with the Everyman hero, the group also pales before the all-absorbing problem of superman before grace.

The organization of the various secret societies in early Heinlein stories reminds one of the Puritan Church of our founding fathers. Within these groups, emphasis is always placed on covenantal relationships. Strangely, none of them is the least bit anarchistic—one might expect it of rugged individualists. On the contrary, members are ever careful to establish, and observe to the letter, all kinds of binding sacraments. The ending of "Gulf," in fact, shows hero and heroine completing their "mission impossible" with a marriage ceremony. They say their vows (a thid listener acts as "witness") as doom rushes upon them. What matter if death do them part at once—a memorial marker is

7

erected on the spot to preserve their union. The pragmatic shaping power of the forms has become the important thing, far more than any mystical core they once may have had.

In Heinlein's latest novels, however, such groups wane beside the rising star of one supreme existence, and we find something comparable to Calvinist "supernatural grace." Election, as in Michael Smith's sudden conversion, overleaps regular channels, elides everything into one epiphanic moment. This contrasts with the early stories, where, if election takes place, it is analagous to what was once called "common grace," the form most amenable to the worldly Puritans because it sanctioned their theocratic order. Its path was visible both in the ritual and social structures of their group—it was God's will incarnate. Indeed, Heinlein's characters in these stories do little more than act out such concrete designs of providence. The thrust of election is both worldly and functional; its result is a firm and efficient social hierarchy.

The roots of Heinlein's basic pattern go deep into the American past. They can be found at that point where the social forces of the Puritan Church and the new mercantile elite of the enlightenment cross and blend, where church member and property owner meet. Indeed, behind the seemingly "democratic" facade of "inner light" grace stands the Puritan theocracy, interpreting their own worldly success as a sign of election. In the same way, behind the Enlightened doctrine of "liberty and justice for all" lies the basic inequality of entrepreneurial society; add this to the sanction of Puritan doctrine, and it becomes incontestable; add a "Darwinian" sanction, and it becomes hereditary as well. Heinlein holds up the same masks of freedom and individual liberty. And yet he despises the incompetent and weak, the democratic processes that enfranchise what he calls "homo sap."

In taking up the juvenile adventure, Heinlein must adopt quite a contrary pattern. However unlikely the channel, through it he taps a tradition that, if not egalitarian, is eminently humanistic. Heroic action at least implies that man makes his way in the world through moral qualities that many humans (not just the happy few) recognize and to some extent possess. The novels in which Heinlein develops this pattern are full of a strange tension. Can the individual help shape his destiny through willed action? Or are deeds futile in a fallen world? Is not election rather irrational and unearnable, a gift beyond all sense of personal merit? Born of this tension, perhaps, is the new emphasis, in Heinlein's novels of the 1960s and 1970s on the ambiguities of election. Out of it rises the new Heinlein hero: supreme man alone before his hidden god.

Critics have admired and condemned many things in Heinlein's work. One of the aspects most discussed is its pretensions as "future history." This study ignores this pattern, because it is both and afterthought and a half-thought. Heinlein wrote the stories, then devised his famous "chart"—only a limited number of works actually fit its confines. Panshin discusses the problems (and artifices) of Heinlein's chronology in detail. Scholes and Rabkin trace the origins of the chart to Stapledon and the tradition of macro-history. In reality, however, Heinlein's ambitions, seen in his rather limited time frame (less than three centuries, or nothing in comparison with man's possible history), and interest in overlapping or recurring characters, are more Balzacian than anything else. So are the manipulators and strong men who people this "epic."

But there are other obvious models as well. Significantly, historical progression is more a family affair than anything else. Movement is by generations: old-style captains like Harriman hand down the reins (gladly and yet reluctantly) to new men like Andy Libby. We are reminded of such *fin de siecle* family sagas as *Buddenbrooks*. Our family here is no typical one, however, but rather the elite of the elect. This aspect is confirmed by the circumscribing presence of the "ancestor," Lazarus Long, whose patriarchial role as father of the chosen people is glorified in Heinlein's latest novel, *Time Enough for Love*. The Future History pattern is interesting but not fundamental. In its imperfection, it is at best a secondary projection of Heinlein's basic rhythm of election and predestination. For want of a better term, call it his eschatological dimension. Its purpose is to set forth on a large scale the same "plan" we see operative in each individual story and novel.

Others prefer to see Heinlein, not in terms of his own History, but in that of science fiction, as a revolutionary. For Alva Rogers, his impact was immediate: his first stories "changed the face of SF in America." In the same vein, Brian Aldiss sees a novel like *Stranger* as the apotheosis of Campbellian SF." This transformation did not, of course, begin here; *Stranger* is a conflation of techniques Heinlein had used in his earliest fiction. From the start, the materials of the pulp tradition became mere counters in his hands, and he manipulated them to new ends. Indeed, it is ironic that Heinlein has been admired for never repeating a formula; the fact is that, beneath his shifting surfaces, he has never had but *one* formula—that of predestination. Over this endless repetition he constructs distinctive episodic, allegorical narratives that have earned him the reputation of a loose plotter and poor "storyteller." In all the praise and blame, however, the essential point is missed. Heinlein gives the old cliches, the insubstantial stuff of pulp entertainment new grounding. For the first time, perhaps, in these early Heinlein stories, American science fiction sinks its roots in a basic cultural pattern, and draws on it for life.

STORIES

Heinlein's short stories belong, essentially, to his early years. From his first published tale, "Life-Line" (August 1939) through 1942, when the war briefly interrupted his writing career, Heinlein worked exlusively in shorter forms, and the medium-length serialized narratives which, in their episodic quality, bear more affinity with the story than the novel. The majority of these early tales appeared in Campbell's *Astounding Science Fiction*; some were written under pseudonyms (the most famous of which is Anson MacDonald). Among this handful of works is some of the most interesting fiction Heinlein has done. In the years immediately after the war (1947-1949), he resumed writing stories—here, however, is a different kind of tale, for a different audience. Where the earlier sketches were often genuinely allegorical—parables in which a complex world view is acted out rather than simply exposed—these are more didactic. More than a change in Heinlein, perhaps, we have a change in audience—the stories were written for the slicks (especially *Saturday Evening Post*) rather than the more specialized pulps. A new tone of sentimentality appears. And in almost all of these tales there are concessions to "human interest." From 1950 on, the short stories diminish. With the exception of a couple of juveniles for *Boy's Life*, Heinlein returns to the SF magazines.

No matter what their intended audience, all these stories share one structural characteristic—they are loosely episodic. This openness fits Heinlein's purpose admirably. Only in the most external sense does a Heinlein story focus on a crucial moment in the life of a character. His protagonists do not, through some process of self-discovery, come to a climactic recognition of identity or place in the world order. Nor are there "surprise endings" in the classic sense, where an ironic twist of fate reveals a man's character to himself. On the contrary, the heroes of Heinlein's tales seem to know from the start what they must do: they face their destiny, accepting it with a singular lack of resistance or self-searching. But there is more here than "doing one's duty": the hero seems chosen, compelled by some inner predilection that goes against all reason or common sense. What the narrative invariably examines, as step by step it becomes visible, is the mechanism of election itself. This can take myriad forms—the more involuted the better—but there is always the same underlying pattern. If the story ends with a surprise, it is the wonder of destiny, always fortunate in some higher sense, if not for its immediate agent. Indeed, the final emphasis is not on the disparity between individual aspirations and the whole, but on their harmony. In amazing ways, the two strands unite, the expendable acts of one being spill over into the larger ongoing process of racial destiny, apparently advancing according to a predetermined plan toward some glorious end. Only in the later Heinlein will that end itself become problematical.

The readers of *Astounding* must have been astounded by Heinlein's first story "Life-Line." Here is a work directly antipodal to the adventure story and its well-hewn plot. Indeed, the center of this sequence of episodes is less a character than a problem. Pinero is more than a model of how we should act. The man and his machine embody a much more general pattern, not of conduct, but of universal law. Instead of enacting destiny, they literally incarnate it. This tale, then, is clearly allegorical. As such it stands, at the outset of his career, as a microcosm of Heinlein's world.

"Life-Line" begins in the middle of a public debate: Dr. Hugo Pinero is defending his discovery—a machine that predicts the length of each individual life span, furnishing exact dates of death—against the disbelief of the scientific establishment. Such an encounter is a Heinlein prototype, and will be repeated again and again throughout his work. Pinero is the unlikely superior being—short, pot-bellied, with dubious academic credentials. His opponent fits the orthodox mold ("America's Handsomest University President"), but is a colossal non-entity. And Pinero challenges not only the conventions, but also deep-seated economic interests: the machine is an obvious threat to the insurance industry.

The story proceeds step-by-step. The first scene exposes the problem, and sets apart the protagonist and antagonists, who will act out its solution in the flesh. Our sympathies are captured by Pinero's rhetoric, as he reverses the accepted views of heroism, and turns the tables on the power structure. In the second scene, Pinero gives technical explanations, and follows these with practical applications: he predicts the impending death of a reporter. The pivot point of "Life-Line" is Pinero's newspaper ad: the scientist crosses lines, setting himself up in business as a "bioconsultant." In doing so, he declares war, and seals his own fate. There is a courtroom scene (another Heinlein staple): forensics replace rhetoric, as Pinero outmaneuvers both his scientific detractors and the hostile business interests which manipulate them. Later, Pinero predicts the immediate death of an innocent young couple, and tries in vain to forestall destiny. The machine is bigger than the man. Finally, there is the scene in which Pinero meets his own destiny—the insurance trust has him bumped off—and its coda: the scientists open the box containing the doctor's predictions of their deaths, together with his own. They verify the correctness of his self forecast, then destroy their own predictions (unopened) by fire.

If "Life-Line" is an allegory, what does it signify? The theory behind Pinero's machine is simple: a human life span, like that of the race as a whole, is a material entity. Each of the "pink worms" that form this "vine" can be measured exactly. More importantly, they may be measured before they end. In this purely physical sense, each individual life is pre-determined. The machine gives man foreknowledge. For the majority, however, this knowledge is intolerable: life is livable only in uncertainty. And yet, Pinero proves that struggle and a clear vision of one's fate are not incompatible. In contrast to the others, he sees the moment of his death and its cause—the defense of his own machine—and still pushes on, meeting his end with calm dignity. What else can he do? Man can know his destiny, but not alter it, as Pinero learns when he tries to save the young couple.

Pinero's machine can be called an instrument of grace only in the most limited sense: it allows each man to know if he is chosen to live. In terms of the machine, of course, everyone dies, so none achieve "salvation" in any form. Heinlein refuses to leap beyond matter—indeed, in later works he explores, obsessively at times, the possibilities of metempsychosis and physical rejuvenation in hopes of extending the ego's existence this side of death. The action in "Life-Line" seems framed by biological determinism. There is the organic analogy of the vine of existence. And it is implied in Pinero's defense of his experimental method that the most viable forms of life are those that best understand the workings of the natural process. Yet within this materialist framework, oddly enough, the Calvinist pattern of election abides. If survival of the fittest is the rule, it is strangely qualified by the presence of the machine. Held up to its baleful light, the idea of fitness itself takes on passive, even paradoxical overtones. Pinero does not survive, yet is fittest because he alone accepts not to survive. The Protestant thrust of this parable is unmistakeable. If Pinero is a new Galileo, the fact he must face is not external but internal—his own destiny. Fitness is measured less in terms of public actions—defense and counter-attack—than private ones. The hero stands apart because he is the only one who accepts the consequences of his acts, who realizes he can neither play god to others nor escape his own predestined end.

Pinero is the prototype for Heinlein's elite man: all are marked by what might called a creative capacity to accept the inevitable. But where does this superiority come from? It is nothing the hero develops—this would imply that any man could do it—but rather something he already has. Indeed, its existence is clearly placed on a level outside commonality. It is not a biological trait in the ordinary sense, for Pinero possesses neither physical beauty nor strength. Nor, apparently, does he have the craft or cunning necessary for blind survival at all costs—if anyone has these, it is his opponents. Pinero puts his great intelligence to a much different end—martyrdom. But it would be wrong to give this a tragic sense either, to see it as protest against a world without transcendence.

Pinero does not elect to die; rather, he is elected. This capacity to accept fate is given to him, not to the others. And this predisposition is awakened by another gift—the idea of the machine. "Life-Line" is not the story of a man conquering his idea. From the first line, he already possesses it—the world is already divided into elect and non-elect. What follows merely confirms this division, and celebrates the wondrous ways of destiny among men. Heinlein may at times imply that biological law sanctions his elite. If we look more closely, however, we see that in Pinero's case such law is suspended. In "Life-Line," there are two states: nature, and a secular form of grace. In the first, "wisdom" is ignorance and darkness; the way of nature is irremediably perverted. Only Pinero is lifted above this: he receives his illumination, and goes to meet his end with the serenity of the elect. His martyrdom is part, not of nature, but of some higher evolution. The fallen state is merely sifted, the chaff abandoned. The destiny of man is that of the chosen few.

The interplanetary job corps in "Misfit" (1939) serves the same function as Pinero's machine—it places all men on an equal footing, so that the new elite may emerge. Young Andy Libby, the protagonist, goes to space with a group of "misfits." Earth is overcrowded, jobs are scarce, ways set; these lads have rebelled against such stifling conditions. A far-seeing policy gives them a fresh start, in hopes that some truly superior being may emerge. He does. Again, from outward appearances alone, Libby would be the least likely choice: he is an awkward, gangling lad from the Ozarks. In Heinlein's parables, our standards constantly fail to discern the elite. Yet, despite appearances, Libby is an intuitive mathematical genius. Answers pour from him compulsively and inexplicably: "Why, naturally the horizon has to be just that far away." There is no rational explanation for his talents: they were given him, and providence allows them to unfold. Libby's destiny fits neatly into the larger one of man's expansion into space. In this tale, he performs the minor task of moving an asteroid—man is rearranging the heavens. He will go on (as we learn in *Methu-*

selah's Children) to invent the space drive that will open up the boundless universe. If things are predestined, they also seem open-ended: already we see a phobia of the end that will haunt Heinlein increasingly in later years.

In this tale, there is the same division between elect and non-elect; it is less radical, however. The common mortals do not see Libby's uniqueness. The more visionary Captain (unlike other established hierarchies in Heinlein, vision usually corresponds exactly with rank in the military) senses it, and explores further. What he discovers has the force of revelation: the hero's full name is Andrew Jackson Libby. All the paradox of freedom in Heinlein lies within this situation. Somewhere in Libby's background is the democratic spirit of individual liberty: in true Jacksonian manner, his parents refused to sign the "covenant." What takes shape in the foreground is an even more select covenant. The link is the name itself. By some strange process of alternate heredty, the spirit of one great man passes into the body of another. In Heinlein, names like Andrew Jackson Libby (or Johann Sebastian Bach Smith) are microcosms of election—the everyman's last name is a mask covering the true lineage of genius. Libby comes into his world trailing clouds of glory. and merely acts out his predestined role. The story has become a ritual more than anything else. The opening scene confirms this: a group of men are being called; at the name "Libby," the hero steps forth and his destiny unfolds.

"Requiem" (1940) is a similar kind of tale. It deals, however, not with a beginning but an end—the culminating moment in the life of the moon entrepreneur Delos D. Harriman, the visionary who first initiated space travel. Ironically, Harriman has never been able to take a trip himself to the Moon. First business interests, and then old age stand in his way. There is a hiatus here: Harriman's destiny is not complete. This story recounts the marvellous working of things that finally allows the gap to be breached, and providence fulfilled.

In "Misfit," a social edict freed men to follow their destinies, to be called or not. But "Requiem" is a story of obstacles. In a series of episodic flashbacks, these are arrayed against the hero's Moon-dream. Father, wife and business partner are unable to believe in him. Now his family has gone to court to have him declared legally incompetent (a favorite Heinlein theme—the old man beset by family vultures—is born). Still, a fortunate paradox prevails, for Harriman constantly loses only to win. The path of destiny is beset with surprises. As a young man, Harriman had been denied, through a reversal of family fortunes, the chance to go to college and become an astronomer. But he will do much better in the end: instead of just looking at planets, he will actually die on one. In the same way, his father had scoffed at his childish desire to touch the Moon—but he will do just that. Now Harriman faces two seemingly insurmountable barriers: ill health and the law. his heart will not stand the trip, and the judge rules against him in favor of his family. A "chance" meeting with two renegade space pilots in an unlikely small-town carnival carries things forward in a manner quite unforeseen. Harriman is denied access to the circus rocket ride because of his heart, only to find men who will take him to the real Moon. The two pilots are also "misfits"—men who chafe under rules and regulations, who seek freedom in space. They take Harriman to certain death. And yet, ironically, their hardness is more merciful than the "concern" of family and friends—itself no more than a mask that hides selfish interests and lack of vision. These men know Harriman (in spite of his social status and physical condition) for one of their own. At the heart of the wider world, a secret group is formed, and pursues its plans in obedience to some higher law.

Even more obviously than "Misfit," "Requiem" is pure ritual of election. Harriman has already conquered space—Heinlein, in fact, will chronicle his struggles in a sequel. Why must he go to the Moon himself? The only answer is that Harriman has not yet experienced grace. His destiny will accept no compromise or compensation—he *must* go. Indeed, the final scene has distinct religious overtones. In wondrous ways, the pains of sickness and space flight cancel each other out. Because he is feeble, accelerational gravity and free fall (proverbially unpleasant to the novice in space) become blissfully dreamlike. Near weightlessness on the Moon makes even death (the most common horror) a thing most fortunate and rare: "He was serenely happy in a fashion not give to most men, even in a long life time. He felt as if he were every man who had ever lived, looked up at the stars, and longed." Harriman is crowned king of this elite. If he (like the speaker in Stevenson's "Requiem" that prefaces this story) also lays him down "with a will," that will has been guided by the predestined plan that fulfills itself here: "He was where he had longed to be—he had followed his need."

" 'And He Built a Crooked House' " (1941) and "They" (1941) belong together in spite of their different subject matter. Both inscribe a pattern that will become fundamental in Heinlein's fiction—a curious polar undulation between center and circumference. It is this rhythm which gradually controls the primal relationship between elected individual and total destiny, linking them together in a closed dynamic system. "And He Built" is the story of architect Quintus Teal, the man with a strange name who builds a stranger house. The tale itself has an odd form: it shrinks to a point, only to expand in vertiginous fashion from it. Things begin narrowing from the very first line: "Americans are considered crazy anywhere in the world." California, however, is their "focus of infection"; its focus is Los Angeles, the center of which is Hollywood, and so on until we come to rest on Teal and his tesseract house. Built for Homer Bailey and wife, the house is a hypercube unfolded into our habitual three dimensions. During an earthquake, it collapses upon itself, into four dimensions. Architect and clients enter this structure, and find themselves trapped at its "center," what Bailey in his three-dimensional logic sees as "the little cube in your diagram that was in the middle of the big cube." Outward from this point new dimensional vistas reach in all directions. They open one window, and look into "inverted" space; open another, and see New York from above.

Once again, a situation serves to separate the elect from those who are not. Bailey's wife is one of those hopelessly frivolous Heinlein females; and he himself is only slightly more able to cope with this strange new world. For both, the tesseract is a maze. Teal designed the house, and understands it mathematically. Nevertheless, he gets out of it not by reason but by instinct. He is different only because he sees the relationship between the two dimensions. The point of contact, the new center, is the mind itself: " 'I watched where I was going and arrived where I intended to.' He stepped back into the lounge. 'The time before I didn't watch and I moved on through normal space and fell out of the house. It must have been a matter of subconscious orientation.' " As with Pinero, it is not the discovery of the machine—the tesseract house in this case—but the ability to face the implications of its working that marks the man. This slightly foolish inventor builds as if he were the instrument of destiny. Even his discovery of the link between dimensions is given to him—he falls out of the house. And what of this faculty of "orientation?" Heinlein gives things a playful twist in the end. A second tremor causes the house to vanish completely. Just before this event, the three had been contemplating the last, and most alien, landscape—a world of yellow sky and tortured shrubs. Without thinking, they leap out the window—and land in Joshua Tree National Monument! In this case, the "subconscious orientation" is most fortunate: vastness and strangeness contract to the familiar California starting point. How do we explain the Baileys' possession of this faculty? Heinlen wryly remarks that all Californians have this reflex. Unique in their madness,this is their saving grace.

In the much different world of "They," there is this same fundamental interplay of center and circumference. "They" is the story of a monstrous case of paranoia turning out to be real—"they" *are* all against him. One of Heinlein's most patently philosophical tales, "They" is nonetheless a chronicle of election in the familiar mode. Once again, the hero is distinguished less by his actions than by a certain disposition to vision. In a perfectly ordinary and comfortable world, he begins to feel alienated. Other people seem ignorant and selfish; he cannot reach out to them, and feels hemmed in by a social wall. One day, by "chance," he pierces a hole through it. He is about to leave the house one rainy afternoon with his wife. He forgets something upstairs, goes back, and opens a window shade—the sun is shining! Like Quintus Teal, he looks out on another dimension. But in this case, clearly, seeing it is not enough: he must discover its relationship to his familiar world. The maze that confronts this hero is epistemological; he is forced back upon his own being as the only possible starting point. This *reductio*, however, is neither Cartesian nor Berkeleyan. He exists not because he thinks, but because he physically is: his five senses are the first line of consciousness, the sole justification for belief in self. On the evidence of these same senses, he cannot dismiss the world "out there" as illusory. He kicks the stone: things really do have physical existence. He rejects both chaos and illusion, isolation and solipsism. The explanation of the world he gives has a strange *a priori* basis, and resembles nothing more than faith. The world simply *cannot* be as crazy as it seems; men *cannot* be *that* indifferent and egotistical. therefore, if the senses are reliable, someone must have made things the way they are. Instead of absurdity, we have the big lie, an adversary: some "puppet master" has robbed

15

these others of their free will. This particular man (who remains fittingly nameless) is given the possibility and disposition to see reality: he is chosen to resist.

In the process of resistance, he displays what is unique in mankind: the dynamic rhythm of an existence that is, in all places and moments, individual and total. Significantly, the hero of "They" never makes contact with another human being. But he is not isolated. The void behind the window shade is offset by a second glimpse at the totality of things, this time in a dream: "Gladness! Gladness everywhere! It was . . . good to know that everything was living and aware of him, participating in him, as he participated in them. It was good to be, good to know the unity of many and diversity of one." In this epiphanic moment, the individual makes direct contact with a new circumferential whole. The result is the dynamic undulation of the many and the one. What these "aliens" do not realize is that the point is as indispensable to this balanced rhythm as the circumference. They are a collective organism that seeks to absorb the individual, to "dismantle" the system. At one point in his reasoning, the hero contemplates suicide as a means of escape from his condition, and then rejects it: to destroy the body is to destroy his sole contact with the external world. His vision of unity is the product neither of reason nor will: it issues again from a "subconscious orientation"—some deeper place where mind is firmly rooted in matter. Nor can the enemy, it seems, tamper with this individuality, or alter it against a man's desire. Some higher law—a "Treaty"—has apparently declared it inviolate. All these aliens can do is study this particular "specimen" as he goes through what seems a series of cyclic incarnations. And they are getting nowhere, are even losing ground: the "creature" who filled the role of his wife has become "assimilated": she asks favors for him the next time around. One is reminded of Heinlein's later Martians, and his other "superior" races: while they sit and ponder man, man's vital existence is busy generating the energy that promises to destroy them.

Heinlein develops a similar pattern in the time travel story, "By His Bootstraps" (1941), but from an opposite angle. Here, rather than election, we have a ritual of damnation. The hero is not merely cast off; he is damned to act out his damnation over and over, without surcease or hope. What occurs is a travesty of election, in which self-awareness is a closed circle, breakthrough to totality a delusion of the ego. The maze in which this hero wanders is that of his own existence. Bob Wilson is writing a thesis on mathematical metaphysics. As he begins to discuss "time travel," a man steps into his room through a "time gate," and tries to persuade him to go back through it with him. A third man appears and seeks to prevent it. A fight ensues, and Wilson is knocked through the gate. Here he meets a middle-aged man who shows him the marvelous Arcadian kingdom he has inherited. He offers to let Bob share its rule if Wilson will help him: he is to go back through the time gate and fetch another man. . . It turns out all four are different temporal manifestations of Bob himself—they chase each other endlessly.

16

The "time gate" seems to be another of these windows into a new dimension. And the world it reveals is apparently as unfallen as that the hero envisions in "They." A second look, however, shows it to be insubstantial, a shadow kingdom filled with childlike subjects and beautiful maidens. Why does Wilson send his double back to fetch books like *Mein Kampf* and *The Prince*? The whole thing is a power fantasy, a creation of the hero's frustrated ego. Indeed, the sole reality here is the circular world peopled by these time-spectres—empty, without beginning or end. If there is a dynamic here, it is not creative polarity, but a cycle of material futility: "You feed the rats to the cats, skin the cats, and feed the carcasses of the cats to the rats who are in turn fed to the cats. the perpetual motion fur farm." The form of the story is circular in manner: it begins with the "youngest" Wilson sitting at his desk, and ends as his "oldest" double sends another back to interrupt this same "youngest" Wilson still sitting at his desk. Throughout the story, the same event is told over and over, each time from the perspective of a different Wilson. The time puzzle is carefully reconstructed, only to be scattered once again as things begin anew. In his thesis, Bob writes: "Duration is an attribute of consciousness, not of the plenum." Wilson's adventures merely act out this solipsistic maxim. Unlike Libby or Delos Harriman, he never reaches beyond self to intersect with some broader order in time and space, never fulfills a destiny. This time the point quite literally absorbs the circumference.

If "By His Bootstraps" is a drama of fate, it is one with peculiarly Calvinist overtones. These time-frames interlock in the most terrible manner to trap their victim; but they are largely mind-formed. Fallen man struggles only to damn himself all the more. Wilson mistakes the gate for a mark of election: actually, he has elected himself. He chafes at the prospect of a narrow life, yearning to escape. the result is his fateful thesis, and the appearance of the gate—projections of his desire. Wilson is not called; on the contrary, what is re-enacted here is the primal sin of intellectual pride. Ironically, once he is caught in the revolving door of time, he grows increasingly vain. Escape is no longer enough. As he works out the intricate relations between the various time segments, he begins to think he sees the ways of destiny, and can outwit it. In spite of all his efforts, man will never escape his fate. But here, there is elation: Bob predicts "a great future." He is and remains a dupe. Neither in the beginning nor in the end does he receive illumination or grace. No matter how hard he tries to reshape his fallen world, he fails. His petty vision at the start predisposes him to "fall" through the gate; the further on he goes, the easier it becomes. This allegory is unique in Heinlein, for it is one of the rare times he traces the destiny of one not chosen. And yet, though the meaning of Bob's adventures is quite clear, Heinlein apparently will forget it in later works. More and more men will come to elect themselves, will turn in paths of their own making that are equally circular and solipsistic. This tale could stand as necessary corrective for a monstrosity like *I Will Fear No Evil*.

"We Also Walk Dogs" (1941) is an interesting tale; here, for the first time, Heinlein focuses openly and unabashedly on a "super group." "General

Services" is an elite society within society. It can accomplish things—and thus act as prime mover in terms of human destiny—because it ignores the laws and customs of weaker mortals. Such an organization is usually the stuff of longer narrative in Heinlein. This version is a short story only by virtue of its limited focus. It is not a climactic moment in the lives of the principals, just business as usual. Nonetheless, the task they are asked to perform is a sizeable one: they must arrange an interplanetary conference on Earth. The problem is gravity. To make each ambassador feel at home, a series of localized gravitational fields is needed. Constructing these fields involves no less than a revolution in physical theory. General Services gets its theory from a recalcitrant scientist. The price—a rare Ming vase located in the British Museum. They steal the vase (we never learn how, but no one seems to miss it); Dr. O'Neil adds it to his private collection without a qualm. They hand Beaumont, the Government Chief of Protocol, a diplomatical and political triumph. Beaumont is well on his way to becoming the first president of a new Solar System Federation. With this stroke, parochialism is struck dead; new visionaries will be needed to lead mankind toward its new destiny. "We Also Walk Dogs" chronicles a day in the life of a growing organism. Before our eyes, the inner circle widens its activities, and acquires a new center. A neophyte is chosen out of the many nameless components of General Services, and proves his worth—Carson becomes one of elect. By the same stroke, Beaumont emerges from the morass of government agencies. But if there is expansion, there is also contracion. The heads of the organization get permission to contemplate O'Neil's vase anytime they like. This point of light, which is the "flower of forgetfulness," becomes their mystical center: "He bent his head over it and stared down into it. . . . It seemed as if his sight sank deeper and even deeper into it, as if he were drowning in a pool of light." In their vital, creative relationship to the vase, we have both the microcosm and power source for the larger dynamic they have just brought into being. Their actions not only have pushed forward the boundaries of the human race, but also secured the center at the same time: Earth will be the focal point of any future planetary union.

"We Also Walk Dogs" provides a transition between the early tales and those written during the years immediately following Heinlein's wartime silence—especially 1947 and 1948. Like the early stories, it is partly an allegory of election, a demonstration of the processes of destiny. And it is partly an exemplary tale as well, one of an openly didactic nature. As it seeks to define the complex relationship between the individual and his universe, it also sets forth exemplary types. We are not only told who the elect are—we are told or taught to admire them. In the three stories published in *Saturday Evening Post* during the year 1947—"The Green Hills of Earth," "Space Jockey," and " 'It's Great to be Back' "—this emblematic quality grows stronger and stronger. Beneath a vague cloak of sentimentality and "human interest," the mark of election not only remains, but becomes all the more implacable and incontestable. These tales no longer offer even the promise of a philosophical problem. Rather, they celebrate a moral universe that is harshly black and white.

18

In its tone, "The Green Hills of Earth" seems an atypical story for Heinlein. It is, however, clearly an exemplum. The form is that of the ballad or folk tale. There is a series of loose episodes, the chronicle of a life organized around one central contrast: we have the official legend and accepted verse of Rhysling the blind space poet, and we have the story of the real man—unkempt and bawdy. To make this contrast is to uncover the fortunate paradox of the artist's life. This insignificant-seeming individual turns out to be a hero as well as a poet—in fact, he is a great poet only because he is a hero. Both his blindness and death—romanticized in the public version—are the results of an unflinching devotion to duty. The fruit of this grandeur and misery is his great poem, "The Green Hills of Earth." As great art unfolds from this unlikely man in unlikely circumstances, we watch the familiar process of election, and rejoice in the ways of destiny.

Once again, in this story there is a narrowing: inside the public shell we find a private core of truth. "Noisy" Rhysling was, in the beginning, just another space tramp—a black-listed engineer with a talent for scurrilous doggerel. He signs on an unsafe vessel, and is blinded while performing (without question or hesitation) an act that saves the ship. His appearance and frivolous words are deceptive. When the moment comes, he does the "right" thing instinctively. Rhysling takes up the life of a wandering minstrel. From blindness, a new vision emerges: the lack of sight mercifully cuts him off from the ugliness of the world about him. On a Mars that has suffered grave ecological damage, he falls back on memory, and in a stroke of fortunate irony, sings about the unspoiled planet of yore. In a sense, he has broken through in his art to a new dimension. Significantly, however, he does not remain here. This circumference shrinks to a new point of reality as the wayfarer makes his first and last voyage homeward. He ponders, in poetic terms, an inversion of things: beauty is no longer the airy towers of Mars but the cool hills of Earth. Improvisation is interrupted by an atomic explosion. Working literally by blind instinct, Rhysling dampens the radioactive material, but exposes himself fatally in the process.

This tale may be read as an allegory. The vast circumference of Rhysling's wanderings—he becomes a symbol of man's restless exploration in space—collapses to a point as he meets his destiny. In analagous manner, human expansion into space—which Rhysling's own acts have themselves furthered in a small but crucial way—suddenly contract in his poetry: we celebrate Earth, the point of return. But the home planet is also a point of departure: from the acts of this blind singer (poetic and heroic), new vision will radiate outward. In its over-insistent association of election with duty, the story becomes dogmatic. Some inner light (the only one he has) reveals to Rhysling the workings of a higher law. These invariably seem to coincide with military codes, blind obedience and sacrifice, which are always virtues, and always beyond the common indication. Indeed, death is not crowned by a public reputation—Rhysling's is swept away in the first paragraph—but by a private act and an immortal product. Again, and in terms of the creative process this time, center and circumference make direct contract; all else is elided.

"Space Jockey" is a more obvious exemplum—and a less successful story. A pilot on the Moon run finds his job interfering with family life. In mid-journey, he ponders the problem, and is on the verge of abandoning his *metier* when an accident recalls him to duty. Not only does he bring the ship through—skillfully and intuitively—but by this act he reaffirms his vocation. He finally writes his letter to his wife: he will remain a pilot and she must follow him. To his surprise, she accepts without hesitation—she was with him all along.

" '—It's Great to Be Back' " is a better tale by virtue of its extreme simplicity. A young couple living in Luna City decide they have had enough of the Moon's confined life—they yearn for the green hills of Earth. In an ironic twist, however, expansion turns out to be contraction. The Earth is cramped and dirty; even worse, the people are rude and stupidly narrow-minded. After a brief stay, the couple becomes tired of references to the Man-in-the-Moon and green cheese, and decides to go back. In a sudden flash of insight, they realize just how different—and elite—the "Loonies" are. To get to the Moon in the first place, it takes a high IQ, and a superior education and disposition. Opening this colony has automatically separated wheat from chaff. The two are accepted back without so much as a test—they are "Moonstruck," and that is enough. Once again, the election process is some mysterious affinity—a stroke of secular grace.

In these latter two tales, the nostalgia of Rhysling's world view is reversed: the center shifts from Earth to Moon. In spite of the displacement, however, the same pattern of undulation abides. In "Space Jockey," the pull of wife and Earthly comforts is broken—in a final symbolic act, she accepts the move to the Moon. Likewise, the stupidity of Judge Schram and his "Junior Rocketeer" son—their "influence" with the high and mighty—are of no avail in stemming this pull away from Earth. The Moon becomes the new center from which man will expand outward. The pilot's actions are vindicated (and Schram's protests brushed aside) by that silent and serene hierarchy who implement this manifest destiny. " '—It's Good to Be Back' " merely celebrates this shift, as do most of the other tales of the period.

"The Black Pits of Luna" (1948) is about a group of silly Earth tourists, and the ordeal of a lost boy on the Moon. We see here what will become Heinlein's stereotypes: the henpecked husband; the weak-willed, fuzzy-brained, hysterical wife (she insists on bloodhounds); the impossible brat. Once again, pressure from above forces the guides to take an underaged and ill-mannered boy on this trip against regulations. During the crisis, parents and other tourists are helpless and useless. Only the older brother (the narrator) keeps his head, and thus perseveres. It is his ingenuity that saves his brother *in extremis*. The moral is clear—the parents are told by the irate guide: "Stay off the Moon. You don't belong here; you're not the pioneer type." The narrator, however, feels a secret desire to return; the guide recognizes him as one of theirs. Again we have a tale of sifting and exclusion.

"Gentleman, Be Seated" (1948) makes the same point in a whimsical manner. An Earth journalist on vacation on the Moon begins probing into the ways of men on the satellite: he thinks there may be scandal or graft in connection with the building of airlocks. What he gets, as he pursues this reasoning, is a very physical lesson in how things work in this different and hazardous world. He is touring a lock in the company of Fatso Konski, "the best sandhog in four planets," when there is a blast and leak. There is only one way to plug it— Fatso plays Dutch Boy with his ample rear end. But he soon succumbs to the cold. The narrator must take his place, and does so without hesitation. All are rescued in the end. More important is the hero's position—the free-floating skeptic has found a most basic point of attachment for the Moon. Is he one of them after all? He sets aside the honor—if Konski wants to collect the chess money he won while waiting to be rescued, he will have to come to Des Moines. Yet, although (as Konski said) he may be "conventional," he has already shown "he has the stuff." This time it is a disbeliever who, in a quite unforeseen way, passes the test of adoption.

"Gentlemen" begins with a discussion of agoraphobia and claustrophobia— fear of the open and of confined places. In terms of the basic rhythm, these represent unbalanced fixations on the point or the circumference. Heinlein's elite, however, must embrace both poles, striking dynamic balance between them: "Make it agoraphiles and claustrophiles, for the men who go out in space had better not have phobias." "Ordeal in Space" (1948) is the story of a man with such a phobia, and how he conquers it. It is a simple tale, and perhaps one of Heinlein's best. During the heroic execution of ship repairs in deepest space, Bill Cole "looks down"—the terror of the void suddenly breaks his nerve, making him unfit for duty. He returns to Earth and a cloistered existence—he cannot look out into open places. A second, redeeming "ordeal in space" comes as the hero spends the night in a friend's high-rise apartment. He hears a cat meowing—it is stranded on the narrow ledge outside. He overcomes his fears, saves the cat, and regains his old calm before the vastness of space. Is this an effort of will? We learn, however, that Bill had an inexplicable affinity for cats— perhaps because they resemble spacemen in their fearlessness and capacity for adaptation. Like seeks out like. Indeed, he is drawn in spite of himself, as if called, to the window, and this foolish and fearful act that will (wondrously) save him. He seems predestined to be a spaceman. Here too, in this story, is the now familiar reversal of priorities. There is the public act of heroism—Bill has a reputation, but it is hollow and useless when the man inside has lost his nerve—and this private one. The cat is both insignificant and all-important. In this contact, the man is revealed to himself, the way prepared for continuation of the grand design. Once again, we have Heinlein's fundamental dynamic in operation. The huge canopy of space contracts to a cat. This is only to pave the way for new expansion: "Little fluffhead, how would you like to take a long, long ride with me?"

Heinlein has written few stories after 1949. These are for the most part afterthoughts, occasional works by a writer who has turned his attention almost wholly to the novel. They vary both in nature and in mood, and can be either harshly pessimistic or sentimental and optimistic. Clearly, the center no longer

21

holds. The dynamics of balance that informed both the earlier allegories and the exempla is gone—in its place, we get apocalypse and apotheosis. Before there was preoccupation; now there is something more like obsession. As such, these scattered tales of the 1950s seem to announce the excesses of Heinlein's latest fictional ventures.

"Sky Lift (1953) is a strange variation on the familiar theme of the call to duty. In an earlier tale, "The Long Watch" (1949), the young lieutenant hero gives his life to save Earth from a military putsch. He dismantles the stockpile of atom bombs on the Moon—and like Rhysling dies of radiation poisoning. Before, Heinlein might have left the act of heroism unsung—after all, during his "long watch," the man has discovered himself, found his true calling. But the private act is no longer supreme. Heinlein gives his hero a funeral procession worthy of Siegfried. Public ritual replaces the inner illumination: the lead coffin must be flown to Earth with pomp and circumstances, so that the best of mankind will be inspired to carry on the fight. "Sky Lift" does not have even the compensatory ceremony. The tale may be a better one in its avoidance of patriotic cliches, but it still remains grim. A cargo of blood must be flown immediately to an outlying base on one of Pluto's moons. To get it there in time to save the diseased men, the trip must be made at intolerably high acceleration—can the crew withstand the sustained high gravity? The protagonist does not volunteer; he is chosen. Through some uncanny insight, the Captain sees in this unlikely hero a special predisposition—what is wanted here is not the traditional ability to act, but a passive talent to endure. He is reluctant—he has a well-deserved leave before him, and is brimming with youthful spirits—and yet he heeds the call. No matter how arbitrary this may seem, it is never questioned. He accomplishes his painful mission, and survives—but in a flash passes from vigor to senility. The focus here is not on the hundreds saved, but on this one wasted youth. In this elided life, Rip Van Winkle is reborn in space. Slowly, in scattered works of this period, a pattern emerges as counter current to the dynamic of formation—that process of growth to adulthood by trial and error which Heinlein adopted along with the convention of juvenile adventure, but with which he was never really at ease. Elision can be macabre, as in "Sky Lift," or it can be a blessing. In a work like *Stranger in a Strange Land*, the young hero leaps in a flash over the responsibilities and anxities of maturity to instant (and unearned) godhood.

"The Year of the Jackpot" (1952) is even more unusual for Heinlein, an apocalyptic vision. as a general rule in his early and middle work, Heinlein presents human destiny as a plan that is both unlimited and endlessly unfolding. In this tale, however, things are cut off by total and irrevocable destruction. Its beginning seems typical enough. In fact, throughout the story we expect something else—survival and rebirth—and we are surprised at the ending. The hero is a common Heinleinian figure: a statistician wanders around gathering data on a series of uncanny phenomena, and patiently plots his curves. Other men think he is crazy, but some fortunate inclination drives him on. He deduces from the study of his graphs and past cataclysmic cycles that

22

this will be "the year of the jackpot"—a mighty convergence of disasters. The hero takes girl and survival gear, and leaves L. A.—just in time, for earthquake, tidal wave, and atomic blast strike successively, engulfing the city. The couple reach a mountain hideaway. In the later novel *Farnham's Freehold* (1964), such a point of survival proclaims itself the center from which a new world will be rebuilt. But not here: the sun explodes as well. A story like "Jackpot" may mark the beginning of a dystopian, constrictive current in Heinlein's work. Gradually, the endless vistas of the earlier fiction will contract around the hero (both *Stranger* and *I Will Fear* are set in narrowly confining—and dystopian—near futures). This new tightness forces him inward on a private world, itself tainted with finality: these later heroes are obsessed with death, preoccupied, not with statistical curves and survival charts, but with artificial prolongation of their own individual bodies.

Odder yet for Heinlein is the sentimental optimism of "The Man Who Travelled in Elephants (1957). Panshin thinks this story was written much earlier. On the contrary, it has neither the allegorical complexity nor the exemplary clarity of the earlier tales. In "Elephants," an old man who has lost his wife is on a bus enroute to one of the state fairs they had followed all their lives. There is apparently an accident. But if the old man is killed, his is a painless death, and an effortless passage into the next world—another time gate or "door into summer." To the hero, this new world is his private vision of heaven—the biggest carnival of them all, in which he and his reborn wife mount their elephants as king and queen of the Mardi Gras. This hardly seems like Heinlein at all. Yet beneath the surface are the familiar patterns. Out of this whole busload, one insignificant, pot-bellied individual is elected, inexplicably to glory. Moreover, he seems predestined to this end. His private joke (and whimsical justification for his fair-chasing) was to say, when asked what line he was in, that he "travelled in elephants." A different writer might have made the elephants of this hero's apotheosis a delusion, as with Hemingway's lion in "The Snows of Kilimanjaro," a moment of dreaming transition between life and death. Instead, fantasy predisposes to a higher reality: on that side of paradise, the hero's vocation is at last recognized—"a fine profession." This story is almost entirely ritual, a huge ceremony of election that terminates in coronation itself. Elided here, in this piece of wishful thinking, is not just an individual life, but the dolorous barrier of death.

Finally, there is "Searchlight" (1962), lone beacon of the sixties, and a slight effort in every respect. A blind child prodigy pianist is lost somewhere on the Moon when her ship goes down. She has no idea where she is. Her rescuers make contact, but cannot use a radio direction finder—they are as blind as she is, or blinder, in fact, as it turns out. The problem is how to locate her. The ingenious solution goes a long way toward confirming the old paradox of the blind who see. A laser beam will be used to carry an audio frequency, a single musical pitch. The general sector of the Moon in which she is lost is divided into a grid of such beams, a span of the 88 notes of the piano. She identifies her note, and is rescued in the nick of time. This is a strange, convoluted tale of election, in which two disparate beings—the blind girl and the unnamed scientist who invents the laser grid—bend all kinds of accepted physical notions ("light can't be heard") in order to effect an all-but-impossible union. The Moon calls for different sense and skills in order to survive. It is as if Betsy, inviable on Earth, has been called to the Moon and subjected to this ordeal solely in order to "see" anew with her exceptional ear. We have all the mechanism for a miracle. When it actually appears, however, it occurs in purely physical terms. As the ship comes down to rescue her, the reborn girl hears it: *"they see her waving!"*

These two people are chosen for this stranger rendezvous, predestined for it by a quality shared in common—personal conviction. Betsy doesn't hesitate to make a concert tour of the Moon in spite of the dangers. As she waits for help which may never come, she remains unperturbed, as if she possessed an even higher sense—that of election. Nor does the scientist hesitate to implement his idea; he even overrides the President of the United States. Out of this meeting come two things: a wider gap between the elect and everyone else, and a promising union of science and art. But if this parable tantalizes us with new vistas, it deceives as well. We have the shell of a blind seer, but no more. "Sight" here, like music, has no spiritual dimension whatsoever. Heinlein expends all this ingenuity only to make a paradoxical shift from one physical sense to another. It is a clever exercise in relative materialism, no more.

NOVELLAS

Heinlein's novellas, simply stated, are that series of longer early narratives written before he began to publish novels. Of varying lengths, the shortest of them are nevertheless more substantial than any of his short stories. Some are quite long, and were originally serialized. Several of these (*Sixth Column, Methuselah's Children, Beyond this Horizon*) were later expanded and published as novels. In spite of this, all these novellas share a form which is peculiarly their own. They should not be considered as something intermediary or transitional, a step on the way to the novel. Theirs is rather an alternate mode of narration. Compared with Heinlein's more orthodox novels of adventure and intrigue, the novellas have a quite different structural logic. The adventure novel is fundamentally synthetic in form; successive episodes are subsumed in the gradually evolving mystery, resumed in the culminating denouement. In the same way, on the private level, the hero's consciousness unfolds in time and space until, at the moment of self-discovery, all previous experiences are encompassed in a flash. Heinlein's novellas often contain numerous episodes. These are organized, however, not in a linear series, but in concentric layers around a single center. In each novella, "action" is restricted to one pivotal problem or adventure. This is rapidly set forth and circumscribed; ensuing events tend to gloss it, building upon this center in analytical fashion. Heinlein's novellas often appear excessively digressive. Indeed, it is this centrifugal structure that generates most of those disquisitive passages

24

that so annoy readers of Heinlein. In each of the narratives discussed here, we do not find linear movement toward a point, but pulsatory movement away from it. The "action" will expand into various satellite realms, and then suddenly (irrationally, if we persist in thinking in terms of linear construction) contract upon the point in order that the story may end.

These early novellas seem to hold the key to the excessively digressive, actionless form of Heinlein's latest work. Does he not, in a novel like *I Will Fear No Evil*, simply overexpand a pivotal situation similar to those found in the novellas? More importantly, however, their structure sheds light on the unusual nature of some of Heinlein's juvenile novels. In certain of these "classics," it seems almost as if this vertical, analytical pattern has been superimposed over the initial horizontal impetus of the action novel. In this way, the "fast starts" we find in many Heinlein novels of the 1950s—where hero and reader are thrown at top speed into the middle of a train of events rushing forward toward denouement—are literally sabotaged. The forward thrust is made to coagulate around a problem center. This may indicate a preference for the novella form; but it does not necessarily mean Heinlein has lost structural control. As we shall see, he can write adventure novels of a more conventional sort when he so wishes. We can only assume, from the persistence of these hybrids, that Heinlein intends this fusion of forms, and is actively seeking some structural advantage from it. Not only are Heinlein's early novellas strongly didactic; they illustrate, in their expansive and contractive structures, a vision of man in which the individual's relation to the whole is predestined and unchangeable. Fusion of this form with the patterns of heroic adventure in the middle novels allows Heinlein to redirect a view of man that must have been basically alien to him. Freedom of individual action, rational control of destiny—values implied in the narrative of heroic quest, no matter how debased—are gradually cancelled out as this axial form spreads from the center of these novels.

The earliest of Heinlein's longer narrative, " '—If This Goes On' " (1940), is also one of the most interesting examples of a form that seems to have sprung fully shaped from the writer's head. Most people know this work in its expanded form (rewritten in 1953 for inclusion in the volume *Revolt in 2100*). The original serialized version is shorter. And yet, in its basic structure, it is virtually the same. The core of both is one single event—a revolution. In this tale, the hero only appears to grow, as he passes from loyal soldier in the Prophet's army to leader of the insurrection against theocratic tyranny. The various stages in his revolt are just so many positions around the periphery of the Cabal. His personal adventures are manipulated to cast light on this complex central phenomenon from numerous different angles.

Panshin calls " '—If this Goes On' " the story of a change of mind: John Lyle is a "man-who-learns-better." If he does so, however, the change comes immediately, at the start of the action. In a flash, a young man eagerly serving one cause is wholeheartedly converted to another: it is but another example of a man predestined to grace. From this moment on, whenever his actions are intuitive, he invariably does the "right thing." He reads the words of Tom

Paine and Patrick Henry, and has a mystical revelation. Heinlein would make us believe that his conversion is not complete: Lyle has been brainwashed, after all, and such barriers to self-realization as prudishness must still be overcome. The process will be slow and painful. There are two ways to exorcise these demons: experience and precept. In reality, each adventure Lyle has on his way to that center of things which is the Cabal is but an excuse for someone to lecture him or us, and in doing so lay open this anatomy of a revolution.

The examples of staged adventure are numerous. At one point, for instance, Lyle is discovered and put to the Question. He doesn't talk; but what difference would it have made if he had? At this stage of the game, he possesses no crucial information whose disclosure might make the action rebound. Nor could this knowledge have been obtained even if he had had it: his mind has been blocked by hypnosis—the narrator now has a chance to tell us how this is done. Lyle doesn't even give his friend Zeb away. But if he had, would this have destroyed the Cabal? The real purpose of this scene is to inform and to reveal. The hero displays the power to resist, to outwit the enemy. We now know he is one of the elect, and are prepared for his subsequent (and otherwise unexplainable) rise in the organization.

In the rambling narrative that ensues, Lyle's adventures as a fugitive on the road serve an informative purpose again and again. After a narrow escape, he hitches a ride with a friendly trucker. His own woes disappear before the marvels of the machine itself: "Nor had I ever been inside a big freighter before and I was interested to see how much it resembled . . . the control room of an army surface cruiser." Is this naivete? Soon we see that all along he has been following a higher plan: "I. . . filed away in my mind the idea that, if the Cabal should ever need cruiser pilots in a hurry, freighter jacks could be trained for the job in short order." As Lyle gradually penetrates the inner organization of the Cabal, we get a guided tour of its workings. Various experts lecture him (and us) on such matters as the conduct of psychological warfare. Good old Zeb mysteriously reappears; Lyle gets a mentor, and the reader a round of digressive dialogues. Zeb, for example, has resumed his filthy habit of smoking. The Puritanical Lyle had always objected to it before—now he openly accuses his friend of sacrilege. He forgets where he is and all he has done. Zeb, however, straightens him out, and in the process proclaims his even more fundamentalist credo: "My religious faith is a private matter between me and my God. What my inner beliefs are you will have to judge by my actions. . . I decline to explain them nor justify them to you." This whole scene is trumped up, against all laws of dramatic construction and consistent development of character, merely to give a pretext for exposing ideas. These in turn uphold without justification the cruel and inscrutable process of election which governs the shape of this narration.

As Lyle reaches the center of his journey, events occur which reaffirm his election. Another old acquaintance miraculously turns up—his old mentor Colonel Huxley, "Head of the Department of Applied Miracles" at his old military academy. Even in that world before grace, there was a strange affinity between these two men. Now Huxley inexplicably promotes this obscure newcomer to a key position in the war effort. This new order, it seems, is just as military as the old—the new army is run right because the goal is right. In Huxley's eyes, Lyle's training in the Prophet's school makes him a prince in this one, where instructors are lacking. Within this inner circle, there is yet another circle which must guide the effort because it is in tune with higher laws of destiny. This celestial chain of command is seen at work in the final battle— the assault on "New Jerusalem." Huxley is put out of action. Lyle should hand the command over to the next officer in line, his own superior in rank. But he knows the man is incompetent: "What would Huxley have me do, if he could make the decision?" Huxley continues to make the decisions. As if visited by his dead commander, Lyle gives orders in his name. The right choices are made and destiny is fulfilled.

Lyle's journey to the center of things is made clear in the most tangible, geographical terms. The Cabal occupies a huge underground cavern in the southwestern United States. But this in turn has a center. It is reached during a picnic excursion the hero takes in the company of Zeb and two girls. With uncanny vision, Zeb guides them through this labyrinth (the passage is "so well hidden that it could have been missed for ten thousand years."). They reach "a perfect small-domed cavern"; here is pristine sand and clear waters—they have rediscovered Eden. In this prelapsarian world, Lyle appears to lose the last of his inhibitions, and thus can tap some vital new energy that will lead him into the battle to come. Such appearances are deceiving, however. At this moment of the center, the hero does not grow; he is chosen. His predestined path is merely revealed to him.

This scene of nude bathing proclaims its purity. In reality, however, what we have here is prurience. Sex is treated exactly the same way as in *Stranger in a Strange Land*. Lyle gazes upon nudity and exclaims: "What is it about the body of a human woman that makes it the most terribly beautiful sight on earth?" He learns at last that they too are human. Heinlein dangles such forbidden fruit before our impossibly naive and prudish hero, and tantalizes him. But things apparently can go no further. An outburst of lust is not possible, for Zeb and the girls only taunt the hero so that they can chastise him all the better. They lecture their charge—but it seems that the lectures are meant for us, because Lyle doesn't really need them. Some marvelous grace preserves him, the "right" woman miraculously appears. Innocence need not be sullied by experience: it overlaps temptation, and achieves perfect union.

In this scene, Heinlein does not reverse the Fall so much as suspend its effects selectively. What we get is a higher form of titillation: Lyle is ever menaced, always saved. The threat may turn out to be an imaginary one. Our hero sees the two girls differently. Miram is a blonde temptress: "I think Lilith must have been a blonde." To gaze upon the other, however, is something else: where Miriam was "naked," Maggie is "merely unclothed, like Mother Eve." Yet Lyle has fears—he believes Maggie is betrothed to Zeb, and now looks on in horror as Miriam draws his friend away for a swim in the raw. This is chimerical, we know: Miriam turns out to be perfectly virtuous—it is just good clean fun. On top of this, there is another unexpected twist: Zeb is not to be Adam after all. Maggie explains: "I am very fond of Zebediah and I know he is equally fond of me. But we are both dominant types psychologically. . . Two such people should not marry. Such marriages are not made in Heaven, believe me! Fortunately we found out in time." This providential revelation saves things—Maggie remains unsullied, and the way is open for Lyle to love her with purity. Or is it? Maggie reminds him Judith exists: she will not fight for him but insists on having him pure. Do we have a real barrier this time? It proves just as ephemeral—Zeb appears and tells of Judith's infidelity (she was too "Female"—"all gonads and no brain"). Lyle and Maggie are obviously destined for each other after all. But if this is the mechanism of election, it has been debased to an insubstantial game, much ado about nothing.

In two ways, both chronologically and thematically, "Coventry" (1940— is a sequel to " '—If This Goes On.' " In this novella, we enter the post-revolutionary world of the Covenant. The religious dictatorship has been abolished. It has been discovered, however, that freedom in society can only extend to a pact in which all freely subscribe. Significantly, this is not called a "contract" but a "covenant." Freedom turns out to be a selective word: as we see, only a certain part of mankind has the need to adhere to this agreement. The rest go to Coventry. Here, supposedly, each man can do what he wants. Yet this is false, for in Coventry anarchy inexorably leads to tyranny—there, in fact, he has three modes to choose from. Man apparently has the option to choose between Covenant and Coventry. But this is not true either. The inhabitants of Coventry, we will learn, are damned, but not by their refusal. A man's fate, in fact, is in no way the product of his actions, but rather of some predetermination. Those who belong are impelled irrevocably by their fallen natures. Yet there are those, like the hero, who make the error, and choose Coventry. Their act does not doom them; rather, it sets in motion the formidable machinery of Heinlein's secular grace. To an even greater extent than " '—It This Goes On,' " "Coventry" proves that, no matter how hard they try, the elect cannot damn themselves.

"Coventry" opens with a problem: to what extent should society regulate individual freedom? David MacKinnon is accused of an anti-social act—he has taken a punch at a detractor: "You believe yourself capable of judging morally your fellow citizens, and feel justified in personally correcting and punishing their lapses. You are a dangerous individual. . . for we cannot predict what damage you may do next." He is condemned to two choices: psychological rehabilitation or Coventry. This scene is cleverly staged, for our sympathies instinctively go out to MacKinnon. In an impassioned defense, he berates his world: lives have become futile and boring because all vestiges of individualism have been stamped out; minds are now controlled and levelled to a single norm. Because the "true spirit of the Revolution" has been betrayed, he will go to Coventry and start over: "I hope I never hear of the United States again." We may believe MacKinnon at first; we will learn how wrong this new way really is.

Heinlein tugs at the "romantic" in us all. His hero (a professor of literature) is one of the last of this breed. He eschews technology, yearns to lead the "simple life." When he goes to Coventry, he takes with him primitive objects—the trust rifle of yore, instead of the modern "blaster." Heinlein is quick to point out the flaw in his logic: "The steel tortoise gave MacKinnon a feeling of Crusoe-like independence. It did not occur to him that his chattel was the end product of the cumulative effort and intelligent cooperation of hundred of thousands of men, living and dead." He later eats a piece of real meat, and vomits when he learns what it is: he is thoroughly adapted to his sophisticated culture, unable to exist without it. In Coventry, he experiences the true fruit of anarchy—lawlessness, impressment, war. He is robbed by corrupt customs officials, and imprisoned by a crooked judge. In jail, miraculously, he meets "Fader" Magee, who becomes his mentor, helping him to escape, and guiding him to the underworld. Once again, there is convergence to a point, contact with a secret society within a society. There is also another rhythm often found in Heinlein—repeated contraction and expansion. Jail cells are often places of dynamic encounter. Dave and Magee team up and stage a spectacular breakout—one of the few moments of action in this story. Once underground, Dave must hide in an old radio-phonograph in order to escape a raiding party. Out of this confinement comes an expansion in a new direction. The hero begins a process of "self-analysis" by which he corrects (one by one) his misconceptions, and initiates the journey back to a world he foolishly rejected.

In this process, though, Dave has a lot of help. While in the hideout, he basks in the parental affections of Fader Magee and Mother Johnson. This brings him to reflect on his own childhood: these people are so warm and understanding that something must certainly have been lacking in his early years. In the true spirit of psychotherapy, he unearths the tyrannical father and condemns him: it was this repressive upbringing that later caused his "atavistic" trait of violence to break out. As he reflects, things are beginning to happen. The ever-warring factions of Coventry, it seems, have buried their differences; they have discovered a new weapon, and plan to attack the "Barrier" and a helpless United States. Fader is wounded trying to get this information to the other side. Though Dave still refuses to go in his place, he takes Fader to the Doctor—and a final round of instruction begins. This lone medical man in Coventry (it seems that doctors are never anti-social) is untouchable, above both law and custom. He is there (he tells us) in "voluntary exile": "He cared nothing for dry research; what he wanted was patients, the sicker the better." He has a young daughter, Persephone, nubile and possessed of god-like wisdom. This creature, young and old at once, is the prototype for numerous female prodigies in Heinlein. Dave falls for this child-like queen of Hades. As she lectures and coerces him, her influence wears away the last vestiges of the hero's social sickness. She informs him of the true nature of the Covenant. It is "the first scientific social document ever drawn up by man." At its core is a

Korzybskian analysis of the term "justice": there is no observable phenomenon in the space-time continuum to which we can point and say "this is justice." Science can only deal with that which can be observed and measured. Something like "damage" is a far more pragmatic measure for human actions. Betrayed in this social logic is a certain Puritanical mistrust of abstractions, and rejection of man's rational ability to manipulate them. It falls back on the predetermined patterns immanent in observable objects. Indeed, Dave's own development, as it follows a parallel path, shows this nicely. The abstract beliefs of the Romantic yield to the concrete facts of experience. These turn out to be merely vehicles for some coherent plan which, in the end, reveals itself as a form of election.

The world of "Coventry" is clearly divided into three state groups, arranged in hierarchical fashion. At the bottom, there are the reprobate of Coventry. Their natures have predisposed them to this Hell. What of the few "good" people we meet there? Heinlein is careful to explain, in each case, that they do not belong. Even the enigmatic Mother Johnson is there by default; she followed her husband, and when he died, simply decided to stay on. As great mother of the underworld, her urges parallel the scientific interests of the Doctor—they are missionaries. Then there is the world of the Covenant. Above this, however, there is a higher circle yet—a select and secret company whose election overleaps the regular channels of the Covenant. Dave is apparently one of these. At last he makes his decision. He crosses the barrier via an underground river. Impossibly, miraculously, he emerges alive on the other side. His rebirth is less astounding than that of Fader himself. The sick man he left behind returns inexplicably as Captain Randall of the Secret Service. As we have seen, Dave's decision to return is not really his own; strong forces guide him all the way. In the same way too, his final act appears no more than a ritual. Fader got out before him—and there were "others" before Fader. In any crucial sense, all these deeds seem insubstantial and inconclusive. The Revolution simply ends; we don't see how it was quelled. It was not destined to succeed, and is not important. All external action pales before the prospects of Dave's election—he will abandon literature and join the Secret Service, becoming one of Fader's higher family of elite spirits. The way to glory is immediate and overleaping. The laws of the Covenant are suspended: he need not undergo psychological rehabilitation. The black sheep is already cured; indeed, he was never sick. In the end the only things that count are the man—"he must ask himself"—and destiny.

In " '—If This Goes On,' " we have a theocracy that implements not God's will on Earth but a Satanic tyranny. The cure for this, in Heinlein's canon, is not unbounded freedom—Coventry is another Hell, where men left to their own fallen natures sink to bestial anarchy. In both these works, an inner group of the elect emerges in order to guide humanity along predestined paths. The novella "Magic, Inc." (1940) is even more pointedly concerned with the emergence of such a group. The original, more revealing title of this story is "The Devil Makes the Law": monopolistic practices turn out to be quite literally the devil's work. The action takes place in a world utterly familiar and contemporary except for one detail—magic. In some mid-sized city of the American heartland, "licensed practitioners of thaumaturgy" operate in harmony with legitimate businessmen to provide services and goods of quality. This balance is upset when diabolical forces begin to prey on human greed and stupidity. But Heinlein is reenacting here neither temptation nor fall—the dynamic is rather one of division. Purposely, he downplays demonic aggression. The adversary is but a shadow, and there is only one belated encounter with it—a long-delayed (and farcical) voyage to the Underworld. Numerous scenes, however, focus on the confusion and folly of mankind. The majority of men are already fallen. Heinlein shows that it takes only a nudge to drive them further and further into the labyrinth of self-corruption. "Magic, Inc." is a narrative of sifting: gradually the true elite, the chosen ones, stand aside and come together. The Satanic pretext is merely the *chiquenaude* that sets things in motion. Heinlein's narrative, more than anything else, celebrates the marvelous ways of a destiny that elects the "right" men to power.

Significantly, the thrust of the action here is neither to defeat evil nor to reform mankind. It is rather (as in "Coventry") to keep things properly divided and in their proper place. Things begin to happen only when these nether forces infringe on the doings of the wrong people. The opening scene illustrates this process. A mafia-style mobster enters the business establishment of Archie, the narrator, and tries to intimidate him into buying "protection" against bad magic. Archie boots him out; the chain of reactions is set in motion. Things happen to his business, he investigates, discovers the tentacular forces of Magic, Inc. He takes his fight through the establishment, and finally outside it. Gradually, in his fight, he gathers about him a circle of unlikely but strong allies. First, he goes to Joe Jedson, rugged individualist, self-made magician, and half a dozen other things. These two encounter, by most propitious chance, Jack Bodie, free-lance licensed magician. Jedson's talents are unrecognized by diplomas; Bodie has the degrees (graduate work at Harvard and Chicago), but eschews them—he learned all he knows from his "old man." A strong alternate current to society's ways is forming; it gathers strength inexorably. From Bodie, we pass to Mrs. Amanda Jennings—on the surface a frail old lady, beneath it a good witch of extraordinary powers. We penetrate a secret world, for which Bodie, with his business cards, is no more than doorkeeper. But if Mrs. Jennings doesn't advertise, neither does her associate, Dr. Royce Worthington, Doctor of Law, Cambridge University. Beneath this dignified exterior there is the old-fashioned Congo witch-doctor. In reality, "Magic, Inc." is a study in comparative power structures. The Chamber of Commerce, in its anarchic disorder, is unable to offer effective resistance to the monopolistic pressures. Each member pursues his own interests, and nothing is resolved. Nor do established legislative procedures fare better. Only this variegated band of individuals can accomplish anything. In a display of power which far outdoes all the public manipulations of Senators, mobsters, chiefs of state, and the infernal schemers themselves, they actually harrow

Hell, hunting down the demon responsible for this operation. They form a taut core within a flabby society. In Hell they discover there is, in like manner, an efficient heart in the unwieldy body politic. Already there, disguised as one of Satan's legions, is Agent William Kane, Federal Bureau of Investigation.

The narrator Archie is the key to this chain reaction. But if such an "average guy" can enter this visionary company, why not any of us? Does Heinlein imply that any man, if he perseveres, can make himself so? Far from it. In a very real sense, this whole process of Satanic subversion is but a contorted form of grace: it exists to elect Archie to the innermost circle. The old form of Mrs. Jennings melts away to reveal an angel. Archie's everyman mask falls, and before us stands her spiritual partner. In his occupation, in fact, there is a possible sign that Archie is predestined. As opposed to the more frivolous forms of commerce and magic, he deals as a builder with "durable goods," iron and concrete. Proof of his destiny comes when some of his companions would turn him back at the threshold of the underworld—this is a job for specialists. But Mrs. Jennings casts straws, and the man who has neither skill nor knowledge in magic is chosen. This whole process has Puritan overtones. A destiny is read in visible signs and objects. Archie's fate is plain to see—the dealer in durables who displays solid (and quite uncommon) courage throughout. No deed he does (or quality he has) explains, however, the final mark of election bestowed on him. The Amanda who goes to Hades is a resplendent young woman—fearful and angelic, but still a shade. When Archie falls in love with her, we think the situation both foolish and physically impossible—sixty years of "real" time separate them. And yet, oddly enough, it is as if this imposed chastity predisposes Archie for union on a higher level. As he sleeps after their journey, the young Amanda comes and plants a kiss on his brow, choosing him as her spiritual lover. The lowest and highest elements of this hierarchy are thus strongly and permanently welded together: "Out present relationship is something. . . to tie to." Here is one of those strange polar groupings of youth and old age which, in Heinlein, cancel all possibility of individual growth between these extremes. Things here remain frozen and static. It is not Joe (the "inveterate bachelor") who will remain single, but Archie. His relation to Amanda holds this society intact: not only do they meet regularly, but they prosper—for Archie, "business is good."

"Universe" and "Common Sense" (1941) form a narrative whole. It is often regretted, however, that Heinlein wrote the sequel to the first story. "Universe" is praised because it ends on a note of uncertainty. We see the ignorant masses, and the hostile power structure; but there is also a small band of determined visionaries which promises to grow. The enemy leader Bill Ertz has been captured: he will be shown the stars—perhaps he will become a convert too. Many feel that "Common Sense" is not only a letdown in aesthetic terms, but a betrayal: why carry the story of this ship/universe and its visionaries to such an end? The sequel, however, is quite consistent with Heinlein's Puritanical vision. Indeed, it is essential to it: the elect must fulfill their destiny, and this second story merely provides (in typical fashion) for its ritualistic working-out. In this light, "Universe" alone is ambiguous. It seems to offer a promise of universal conversion: "Why, then we shall just have to do it all over, I suppose, till we do convince them." "Common Sense" proves this impossibility a Romantic dream. In this novella, the group fails bitterly in its attempt to reform the whole ship: humanity in general proves itself unregenerate and fallen, hopelessly blinded by "common sense." Characteristically, they are not converted but abandoned. The ship is left to continue its benighted path; the small band of visionaries go off to begin a new existence on a virgin planet. The meaning is all to obvious here. Their knowledge is rudimentary, heroically insufficient; the amazing "luck" that guides them is, visibly, the hand of destiny.

As with all these early novellas, the opening scene of "Universe" plunges us less into intrigue or action than an alien and problematic world. This story is one of Heinlein's triumphs of "extrapolation." A whole mode of human existence, at once strange and all too familiar, is skillfully built up of rapid touches and crucial details, as we catch it in mid-evolution. On a starship of the Jordan Foundation, bound for distant Proxima Centauri, there is a mutiny. The result of this struggle is reversion to a cultural dark age. To the survivors, the ship becomes their universe. A new cosmology is created: scripture ("the Lines from the Beginning") springs up telling of "Jordan's Plan," of the creation and fall of man. In this account, Chief Mutineer Huff becomes Lucier—Heinlein gives us a masterly-drawn example of the human mind creating its myths out of limited knowledge, and thereby confining itself to the narrowest space. The society of "Universe" is thoroughly medieval in its "geo-centrism." Men inhabit the lowest areas of the ship, where gravity is highest. Their culture is divided into two classes: the peasant-serfs, and the "Scientists," a priestly caste whose "science" is purest scholasticism. The upper, low-gravity levels of the ship have been abandoned to the "muties"—mutants caused by radiation resulting from the destruction of the protective shield. Typically, the Scientists' explain the muties not in physical but symbolic terms. They are the cursed descendents of the "mutineers"—the outcast race. To man, then, the sky is closed. And yet, only this way lies salvation, for here one can look out on the stars, see this "Universe" for the insignificant thing it is. The desire to go up remains in the human race. This story opens with a foray by three boys into the dangerous realms above. For two of them it is sport, an adventure. For the third, however, it is more: Hugh Hoyland feels a strange, inexplicable sense of awe. In this dark world, he is to be the new Galileo. Called to seek the higher truth he intuits, he will look out on new worlds.

But are the muties really the more fallen race? In "Universe," the matter is far more complex. Deprived of the possibility of raising their own food, the muties have reverted to a nomadic tribal existence, living off foraging raids and practicing cannibalism. And yet, however grisly, their use of the dead seems more natural than man's. The humans below feed their departed (as well as live prisoners) into the mass converter. The ship is providentially kept on course. Ironically, however, this is not their intention at all. In their superstitious ignorance, they cannot imagine the true purpose of the machine. It has become a Moloch, its function solely ritualistic. The muties are made practical by their need to survive. This same self-reliant existence also leads the best of them to a genuine intellectual detachment. At the center of "Universe," is the fortunate encounter between Hugh and Joe-Jim Gregory, the two-headed mutant "philosopher." Hugh is captured while on one of these "reconnaissance" climbs. But rather than eating him, Joe-Jim spares the boy and keeps him as intellectual company. Before his capture, Hugh had been only potentially a rebel. He might ask his old teacher, Lieutenant Nelson, why the sacred texts referred to the ship as "moving," and not be satisfied with his casuistical answers. In spite of these doubts, he remained a prisoner of his world's superstitions. Joe-Jim, however, offers new vistas. His logic batters down these barriers. Then he takes Hugh and shows him the stars. But if Joe-Jim is keenly intelligent, he has a flaw: he is by native temperament an intellectual, a bystander, an observer. He is interested in the "how" and the "why" but his will to action is satisfied with comfort and convenience alone. Once Hugh sees the stars, he wants to reach them: "Why don't we finish this job?" He strikes a pact with the reluctant Joe-Jim, and a coalition of mind and will is formed.

Joe-Jim is detached, but he is not a solo. He operates with a band of devoted braves who, in action, are capable of heroic loyalty. Virtue is not entirely dead down below either. Hugh returns to high-weight to spread the news, and is condemned for heresy. Of all his former friends, only the peasant Alan Mahoney comes to his aid. We wonder why, and so does Alan—he understands nothing of Hugh's ravings. Hugh calls him, and he comes; following some irresistible inner urge, Alan does Hugh's bidding, undertaking the perilous climb to Joe-Jim, and persuading him to rescue his ally. In this story, a series of gradually narrowing circles form and replace each other. At the heart of these respective societies, each hero shapes a world within a world. As they unite forces, an even tighter circle is formed, the center from which this new push to the stars will emanate. As this innermost sphere is shaped, there is a certain balance: Alan's blind devotion to Hugh mirrors that of Bobo the dwarf for his master. The purpose of Heinlein's sequel is to show that this equilibrium is not only unstable but transitory. The final circle of the elect has not been reached. this group will inevitably break down and reform—and when it does, the muties will have no place in it.

In "Common Sense," balance turns out to be paralysis—a dichotomy that cannot generate vital energy, but only freeze things in hopeless stasis. The dialectic between what are essentially realist and nominalist views leads nowhere. Already in "Universe," the allegorist interpretations of Nelson were offset by Ertz's matter-of-fact vision: "The ship was the ship. It was a fact, requiring no explanation. As for Jordan—who had ever seen him, spoken to him. What was this nebulous plan of his? The object of life was living. A man was born, lived his life, and then went to the Converter." This opposition only. hardens in "Common Sense." The sterile patterns of human reason cannot be broken—they must be abandoned, and with them the mass of mankind. Interestingly, Joe-Jim literally incarnates this fatal division of the human intellect. His lack of will and purpose is the direct result of his doubleness: as his heads carry on their futile discussions, he becomes inoperative. True, Heinlein gives Joe-Jim a glorious death in action. We note, however, that the mutant performs heroically only after he has lost one of his heads.

Physically, Joe-Jim is part of fallen, unregenerate mankind. As such, he must be excluded from the company of the elect. This is accomplished by the fantastic train of events in "Common Sense." The story begins with the miraculous conversion of erstwhile enemy Bill Ertz, and ends with the departure of this small band of visionaries for a new planet. At the very last moment, as they are menaced by a new ship's rule bent on destroying them, they discover an auxiliary space craft—incredible good luck. They guess, by another fortunate insight, that they are entering an alien solar system—this must be the end of the trip! The treachery that forces them to abandon the ship, as it plunges blindly through Proxima Centauri, is a blessing in disguise. They do not really know where they are going, but luck enables them to locate and land on a planet that (incredibly) turns out to be inhabitable and peaceful. There really is too much "chance" here. Heinlein is openly showing us destiny at work; there was a "Plan" after all, but quite a different one from what the Scientists imagined. It includes the muties only in a limited sense. Joe-Jim is a necessary step in the process, but clearly he must be surpassed. His mutation, we learned in "Universe," was most fortunate: "Had he been born two normal twins and among the crew, it is likely that he would have drifted into scientisthood as the easiest and most satisfactory answer to the problem of living." Destiny uses this exceptional creature, but must dispense with him in turn if a higher stage is to be reached. Like all his kind, Joe-Jim is genetically inviable. Hugh, Bill and Alan, aware somehow of the role they must play, drag women along with them—faceless creatures, obviously chosen for breeding purposes. By some higher law that watches over racial purity, the mutant heroes must die. Alan remains; Bobo, the nobler in many ways, perishes. Joe-Jim dies heroically—and yet in the end, the world of action and adventure turns out to have only secondary importance. These noble acts are transitory, another step only in that sifting process that gradually isolates the select few destined to carry the human seed to glory. The ways of Heinlein's providence may seem incredibly tortuous—man has regressed, struggled, erred. Yet we must remember that this is not all mankind, but only a ship. And of its number, the "right" few do reach their destination, on time, and perhaps under better terms than would have been possible otherwise. Destiny has reserved for this handful of survivors—and because of their limited numbers—a return to innocence, a new Golden Age: "From now on, Alan always Good Eating."

Finally, there is "Waldo" (1942). This Anson MacDonald story is, in a sense, Heinlein's archetypal novella, and one of him most complex and provocative allegorical statements. In the intricate interplay of center and circumference, in the gradual reduction of the external world to a creative polarity between this young, isolated super-genius and an old hex doctor, "Waldo" traces configurations that will later be worked out in *Stranger in a Strange Land*. The later novel will simply expand these basic patterns, and develop them in terms of linear intrigue and *Bildung*.

There are several elements to this strange tale. Its core is the fairy-tale motif of the monster who gets a human body. Heinlein gives this a twist, however, which links it with the recurrent theme of election. Waldo's is not merely a case of the beautiful spirit purifying and uplifting an ugly body. Instead of unbroken elevation, the pattern here is rather that of the fortunate fall. With his extreme *myasthenia gravis*, Waldo is literally the prisoner of gravity. Through a feat of intellect, he compensates for this by creating his weightless home in the sky. Instead of curing man's fallen state, human intelligence only worsens the original rift. This space home is alternately "Freehold" or "Wheelchair"; Waldo becomes a great floating brain in the middle of a spherical room. He must fall again in order to rise, must touch Earth. He despises those "nameless swarms of Earth-crawlers," and yet is shown just how dependent on mankind he really is. It is in falling to Earth that he paradoxically liberates himself from this dependence. He makes contact, not with the mass of men, but with his elective counterpart among it—Gramps Schneider. Out of this creative union, Waldo rises a whole being. Indeed, only because he resolves his own plight can a solution to the general human condition be found. All mankind is succumbing to *myasthenia*, suffering the radical split between order and chaos. In this Waldocratic universe, however, the general cure is only a secondary development, an offhand gift from the recipient of grace to those not chosen.

Central to "Waldo" is the symbol of hands. These are constantly (and in various forms) reaching out, touching, physically uniting two apparently sundered poles, establishing a current of creative energy between them. This image unites the several levels of action in the story into a cohesive network. There is Waldo as a special man, reaching vertically out to his predestined point of contact on the circumferential human world. There is Waldo as fallen man, reaching laterally into "Other Space," and drawing the energy which miraculously lifts him (and humanity) up again. And there is Waldo as partial man, reaching horizontally across his own arrested growth in order to draw this emotional child to instant maturity.

The incredible web of interlocking circumstances which is "Waldo" is radial in form. In its dynamics, however, it is centripedal, not centrifugal. At the center is Waldo F. Jones. Converging on him are two separate, apparently different problems. On one hand, there is engineer Jim Stevens of North American Power-Air, with their "radiant power" reactors that don't work but should by all the known laws of physics. On the other, there is Doc Grimes, and his theory of the general physical debilitation of mankind. At the center, we learn that these stands interrelate—they are two forms of some general power failure. But even when the connection is made, a seemingly impossible quandary remains. "Progress" has led to the creation of radiant energy. This weakens men and weak men in turn affect the power of their machines and cause them to fail. Once again, fallen man wanders lost in the maze created by his own intellection. The energy loosed into the world is leaking away somewhere—but where is this point of drainage, impossible by current notions of physics? The tightness of this infernal circle precludes any hope of returning to a prelapsarian state. But if it cannot be broken that way, it can be balanced with some new element, so that the ongoing polar dynamic of change in permanence may continue. This requires an act of grace, the sudden opening of a door into elsewhere. And grace does not touch ordinary men. The hidden door, we learn, was in the mind of man all along: here is both the leak and the power to rechannel it. But this discovery is made in one great mind—Waldo's.

Waldo undertakes to solve the problems Grimes and Stevens bring him. He does not do so, however, out of altruism or out of egotism—this invasion of his sealed world makes him perceive his own condition in a new light. He is suddenly aware of the fundamental inbalance his isolation has created. To overcome gravity, to suspend oneself in weightlessness, is merely to move from one extreme to another: sterile oscillation. Before, Waldo had been the suspended brain who regarded all humanity as his "hands," and who actually reached out through his various mechanical extensions (he calls them "Waldoes") to manipulate men. His position is that of tyrant. Suddenly, he discovers that he in turn is helplessly dependent on the creatures he controls. This polarity is mutual enslavement; to break out of it, he must establish some new vital contact with the Earth he has forsaken. He goes to Gramps Schneider, the mysterious Pennsylvania hex doctor, and a dynamic nexus is established. The two dwellings are polar opposites: Schneider's quaint old house is as Earthbound as Waldo's is detached and rootless. The symbol (or sign) of their creative interplay is the gravity-operated cuckoo-clock: one ticks in Gramps's house; the other is built and operated by Waldo inside a gravity shield in his floating home.

As the Schneider-Waldo axis is forged, the image of reaching hands takes on new significance—the grip of tyranny becomes fingers groping after creative union. The "de Kalb generators" hexed back into operation by Gramps have antennae that reach out like hands. These extend (he tells us) into "Outer Space," and draw their power there. Furthermore, he repeats this "laying on of hands"—he strokes the machine in the "right" direction—on Waldo himself. Then too, Waldo is told he can extend his mental hands and take strength there. For a brief instant, Waldo feels a surge of power against his prison of gravity. This, however, is a revelation, but no miracle cure. It simply sets in motion the rhythmic undulation of a new creative process, and dynamic connections are made between formerly antithetical values: the individual and selfless energy, science and magic. Schneider, in fact, has a very Emersonian vision of "other space": its power is not to be sought outside the self, but is rather "inborn," part of the mind itself. Gramps's view is metaphysical; Waldo on the other hand, insists on locating this place topographically. He sets out in his laboratory to explore this new dimension physically, to map it, and in doing so literally colonize it, shaping it in accordance with his own conqueror's will.

Only at this physical center of things can he tie all the various strands together. The machines failed, Schneider stated, because their operators were "tired." Waldo translates this into scientific terms: if energy is "shorted" somewhere, and if this "Other Space" is where it goes, then could not the point of contact be physically in the mind? If men indeed suffer from generalized, radiation-induced *myasthenia* (as Doc Grimes thinks), perhaps the mind is leaking into another dimension. Using smaller and smaller mechanical extensions, Waldo is able to reach physically, surgically, through the brain to the portals of this "Other Space," and thus verify his hypothesis—the synapses are the point of contact.

Discovery of this link leads to some important speculation as to the nature of this other dimension: "If the neurological system lay in both spaces, then that might account for the relatively slow propagation of nerve impulses as compared with electromagnetic progression. Yes! If the other space had a c constant relatively smaller than that of this space, such would follow." It is but one step from imagining an alternate universe to actually creating one: "The Other World was a closed space, with a slow c, a high entropy rate, a short radius, and an entropy state near level—a perfect reservoir of power at every point, ready to spill over into this space wherever we might close the interval." In Gramps Schneider's mystical vision, the world varies according to the way one perceives it: hence, "a thing can both *be*, not *be*, and *be anything*." But this, as the mad Dr. Rambeau proves, can be chaos. Out of chaos, however, Waldo opts to bring cosmos: "He cast his vote for order and predictability! He would *set* the style. He would impress his own concept of the Other World on the Cosmos!" If the individual replaces God, the creative polarity that selects and guides him insures that he will do the same thing that God would have done. Waldo's "own" idea is directed by some higher plan, the "style he sets." The new nexus he establishes, merely restores the dynamic interchange between center and circumference: "I think of the [Other World] as about the size and shape of an ostrich egg, but nevertheless a whole universe, existing side by side with our own, from here to the farthest star." It is from this super-position of polar opposites that the solution to the practical problems comes: "Start out by radiating power into the Other Space and pick it up from there. Then the radiation could not harm human beings." This magical engineering may save mankind's health and economy, but it remains simply a by-product of the real drama of Waldo's election.

But this universe maker remains apparently bounded by his own physical body. Yet his weakness also proves an illusion, a veil which falls to reveal the real Waldo. To Gramps, the solution is one of incredible simplicity—reach out your hands. Again, Waldo sets out to recreate metaphor in literal, physical terms. He has explored the brain with mechanical "hands," the waldoes. Why then can he not use his mental "hands," the nerve synapses, to reverse this process of leakage, and draw power like the vitalized antennae of the de Kalbs? he measures his new-found strength, significantly, in the most tangible way—with hand grips. His passage from weakling to giant also involves another form of reaching out: he floors Jim Stevens with one surprise punch; in an instant, the callow boy becomes a "man." Because Waldo is a scientist and not a hex-doctor, we may think we are witnessing an act of conscious will. Actually it remains a miracle cure. Gramps reveals a higher truth; as he translates this into new terms, Waldo does no more than act out a predetermined pattern of grace. He does not grow, either in the physical or the emotional sense; he is transfigured.

In spite of this, however, election in Waldo's case is a centripedal process. He breaks out of initial isolation only to achieve a higher form of oneness, in which the circumferential world itself is gradually absorbed by the center. The story line is a closed circle—it begins and ends with the resurrected Waldo performing his tricks and receiving homage from his admirers. The ruler of two worlds—this space and the other—is the alpha and omega of the linear narrative as well: all poles close in him. As these two spaces (through the paradoxes of topology) do not coincide, and yet do, so Waldo executes his feats simultaneously in both the micro- and macrocosm: the neural surgeon probes the infinitely small, the acrobat defies space and gravity. Gramps Schneider is gone: the initial contact was all that was needed. From that point on, everything external is gradually drawn to the center, transposed upon it like a looking-glass. First and last in this story, we have a vision of unity that is solipsism—self mirroring self. Waldo can look out on the world of men with perfect serenity ("such grand guys") only because they have become perfect adulators. In its convolutions around an absorbent center, "Waldo" looks forward to *Stranger in a Strange Land*.

TWO NOVELS OF INTRIGUE

Heinlein's early tales and novellas are perhaps best treated as allegories. To critics, his latest "philosophical" novels also have seemed parables of the same sort—different only in that they are more protracted and offensively didactic. It is tempting to leap in this way from early works to late. However, this slurs over important differences between the two periods. The emphasis in *Stranger* and its progeny has definitely shifted. The collective group may still be present, but the individual hero now takes precedence over it. In parallel fashion, epiphanic grace—direct contact between this individual and the predestined plan itself—supplants the elaborate machinery of common grace. If there is still interest in the problem of covenants, or the workings of elect groups and societies, it is now secondary to the emergence of a super hero. Moreover, such a leap obscures the fact that this shift is the result of a natural process—one that occurs subtly yet pervasively throughout Heinlein's novels of the 1950s. It is possible that this change in structural and thematic emphasis stems from tension on the narrative level itself. On one hand, there are the conventional patterns Heinlein inherits along with the particular form of adventure novel he adopts—intrigue and initiation. In his early tales, if these appear at all, they are embryonic at best. On the other hand, there is Heinlein's own belief-impelled logic of storytelling, fixed and immovable from the start. At many points, these are mutually exclusive. Are deeds, for example, to be meaningful or inconsequential? Are they essential to the outcome of the action, or superfluous to it? Does an individual become a hero through interaction with events, or by resisting and defying fate? Or is he chosen, shown to be part of some higher plan irrespective of his decisions and desires? Throughout the period of the juveniles, the Calvinist base refuses to yield. The result of this friction is the gradual alteration of the conventions of intrigue and initiation. In novel after novel, the hero only appears to be the product of his acts. Enemies are defeated, men come of age—but these only seem to result from individual effort. More and more, there are ellipses, inexplicable changes of state. Subtly, will is replaced by predisposition to election, the process of formation by that of memory. The hero becomes not what he makes himself but what he was all along, hidden until the inner self is finally revealed.

In practice, the patterns of intrigue and initiation are inseparable. Yet for the sake of analysis we must cut them apart. Episodic adventure in Heinlein is invariably shaped by a particular kind of intrigue. A problem arises, in the form of an aggressive enemy cabal, some secret society that seeks to usurp power. The actions of this false group force the true body of the elect to form, and to enter into protracted battle, until the last of the enemy is destroyed. Development is linear, and apparently causal. In contrast, a novella like "Gulf" (1949) is an anatomy of election. In the long, static central section of this tale, the rules and rituals that bind this company of supermen together are dissected with meticulous care. Intrigue here is only a framing device. In the beginning, it serves to position the hero, bringing him to the jail cell, and his fortunate (and inexplicable) meeting with Kettle Belly Baldwin. The "gulf" in this tale is that of election, and in this confined space the hero crosses it. Quite literally, he sees the light: he reads Kettle Belly's cards, and is liberated. His newly found freedom, however, immediately contracts to the rigid discipline of this secret society's "training camp." Mastery, in turn, will lead to boundless power. Following a strangely literalist interpretation of Korzybskian semantics (human though is performed only in symbols), the ability to learn "speedtalk" becomes a mark of superiority: "Any man capable of learning speedtalk had an association time at least three times as fast as an ordinary man. . .a New Man had an *effective* life time of at least *sixteen* hundred years, reckoned in flow of ideas." Nevertheless, these supermen seem to share with all mankind the common legacy of the Fall: "We are not like them; but we are tied to them by the strongest bond of all, for we are all, each and every one, sickening with the same certainly fatal disease—we are alive." But does this bond hold them? At the end of this story, the flagging intrigue is revived to illustrate how chosen men transcend this "sickness." Election is more than a matter of intellect or even physical strength—the hero is not super intelligent, and Baldwin has his belly. It is, ultimately, the power to make the act of faith, to give one's life without asking why. Mrs. Keithley and her diabolical plan to rule the world reappear. In the short scene that closes "Gulf," there is a flurry of schemes and ludicrous maneuvers—but the effect they produce is the opposite of suspense. The hero's deeds are an afterthought—and by the same token, his death is painless—because the result is a foregone conclusion. His final act is less important than the plaque that commemorates it.

The novella that comes closest to prefiguring the novels of intrigue is "The Unpleasant Profession of Jonathan Hoag" (1942). Yet even here the resemblance is only partial. The hero and heroine, a husband-and-wife detective team, are drawn by their strange client Jonathan Hoag into struggle with the mysterious "Sons of the Bird"—men who dwell beyond the looking glass, and believe themselves to be fallen angels, hence the rulers of mankind. As it turns out, this action is only a facade. In "Hoag," events must be read allegorically—in fact they can be read no other way. Readers are often put off by the futility of the detectives' efforts: nothing they do has any impact on the enemy. But the reason for this is simple: this intrigue is not the central concern of the story. The real mystery is the identity of Hoag himself. The protagonists do not discover his identity; Hoag reveals it to them himself in the end. His profession, and the fate of the Sons of the Bird, relate to the detectives' efforts in a way which is oblique and symbolic. Hoag is an "art critic." The creation of our world, it seems, is the apprentice work of some celestial art student. But he "painted" it wrong—the Sons of the Bird are an error, and should not have had human form. It is the critic's job to judge the work—can the flaws be corrected, or should the whole thing be scrapped? Such criticism, however, cannot be abstract connoisseurship. The only way to judge this creation is by becoming part of it. Though Hoag takes human form, his being remains split. The two halves remain apart until the heroes' bumbling insistance forces them together. Theirs is a blind but fortunate drive. Hoag's contact with the Randalls miraculously provides him with the right "perspective," and mankind's worth is seen and spared.

As it turns out, this tale of intrigue is really one of Heinlein's most intensely Calvinistic parables. A divided and fallen world is created by some aloof and indifferent artist—he is "hasty or careless." The existence of the Sons of the Bird springs from this primal error: their grotesque forms were "painted over" with those of men. The original fault is division and it is not mended here—the "painting" is not thrown out. On the contrary good appears out of a more radical schism. We see the ever-recurring drama of damnation and salvation: the reprobate are separated from the elect according to some predestined plan. At their origin, the Sons are deformed; giving them human bodies does not elevate them, but brings them to damn themselves all the more. In their "stupidity and arrogance," they give in to what is essentially the sin of intellectual pride. Like the survivors of the mutiny in "Universe," they too forge a cosmology to sanction their blindness: "In the beginning was the Bird." The Randalls also wander in the dark. And even Hoag, in taking human form, leads a split existence. Destiny, however, brings these two together, and there is light. At this point of revelation, the Manichean struggle simply evaporates. There is no mighty battle; the adversary is now seen as he always was—an illusion—and the elect are instantly and effortlessly transposed to another plane of existence. On both sides, there is the flash of understanding. Hoag recognizes the tangibles of this world—food, drink, this couple's love for each other—and judges: "good art, good art." The dynamic solidity of mankind, however, is the product only of a chosen few, people like the Randalls. What better image of election could there be than their ride through Chicago to escape Hoag's eradication of the Sons of the Bird? With the window rolled up, the city is there; when it is rolled down, all is void. They have become the center of things, and one from which a new life beyond the Bird will begin. But why are the Randalls chosen? They are largely ineffective, their love (as Hoag sees it) is "tragic"—they too are mortal. Grace is always mysterious. And yet, in a sense, they possess certain native qualities that predispose them to it. Most of all, their blind courage to continue leads them to discovery. Long before Hoag's disclosure, they come across the illusory nature of their enemy. On the plane of action, they cannot defeat the Sons of the Bird. But by hanging mirrors, they simply blot them out. Hoag's role is essentially revelatory—he tells them the meaning of the things they did before in inspired ignorance: "Profession" may be a fascinating allegory, but it is hardly a tale of adventure and intrigue.

In Heinlein's novels of the 1950s, however—both the juveniles and those rarer ones with older heroes—intrigue plays a much bigger role. The two seminal works in this regard are *Rocket Ship Galileo* (1947), and *The Puppet Masters* (1951). In *Galileo*, as in the early tales and novellas, there is a problem to solve, a technical feat to be accomplished: a rocket must be built and flown to the Moon. Ostensibly, the motivating force in this case is not the problem itself, or even that predestined plan that brings men to accomplish it in wondrous ways. There is an aggressor: a group of Nazi survivors want the Moon for their own evil purposes, and seek to prevent other possible flights. What brings this unlikely circle of heroes (young and old) together, and prods them into functioning as a unit, are tangible acts of espionage, sabotage, and violence. *Galileo* is one of the rare Heinlein works in which an "enemy" (however trite and contrived he might be) actually continues to operate from one end to the other. *Puppet Masters*, on the other hand, is the archetypal example of "adult" intrigue. It is not a novel of inner growth, but of external advancement: the attack of a hostile and alien control network forces an individual member of an already hyperselective secret agency to move up the chain of command. He passes from subordinate to leader, and a new and tighter inner core is formed. But this distinction between juvenile and adult novel, seen in the light of intrigue, turns out to be artificial. Not only does intrigue have the same function in both of these works—to give linear impulsion to the process of election—but each has basically the same kind of intrigue. In *Galileo*, very adult Nazis are handled childishly; while in *Masters*, the old fairy tale theme of vampiric possession (the "slugs" even leave red marks on their victims) is given an adult air of international menace and racial disaster.

If there is difference between these two seminal works, it lies on another plane: they represent two contending patterns—the emergence of the group, or the emergence of the chosen individual; the third person narrative, or the first person narrative; incorporation into the collective entity of the elect, or detachment from it. Beyond this, however, in the context of these novels of intrigue, there is a higher similarity in the way each strain develops over this decade. In both, the patterns of intrigue themselves are gradually emptied, made to conceal a sudden (and often dizzying) expansion of the old static center. The distance between *Masters* and *Starship Troopers*, for example, is great. In spite of a certain laxness in the causal net, the former remains a tale of intrigue. The hero's advancement is bound throughout (at least on the surface) to a purposive chain of events—continued conflict, the necessity for action. In *Starship*, however, a very similar intrigue (the enemy here is parasitical and non-individual as well) is delayed until the end. The battle scene becomes, as in "Gulf," an illustrative episode. In "Gulf," though, intrigue is revived on the rebound, as an afterthought. In *Starship*, the presence of an enemy and a war "out there" is used to create "suspense"—a leaning intended to give vector to the long period of indoctrination which has become the real heart of the story. The central scene of "Gulf" is an open dissection of the mechanics of election. That of *Troopers*, under the guise of necessary training, deals more with the mysteries (and injustices) of individual, overleaping grace. The presence of an unquestioned goal—the suspended promise of intrigue—disguises and softens this dubious emphasis somewhat.

The distance between these two novels is less than that between *Galileo* (or a much better work in the same vein, *Red Planet*), and *Tunnel in the Sky* (1955). All have basically the same thematic configuration: the pressures of an external situation causes an inner circle of youthful heroes to form. In *Red Planet*, however, intrigue remains a real shaping force. Greed and tyranny must be overthrown, and the boy's efforts contribute to this. There is, of course, fortunate paradox as well: the Martians must threaten to destroy all men before the bad ones can be eliminated. But the boys' actions are in part responsible for this "philosophical" ending, where judgment by a higher power suspends the contending forces. Not only have they finally stirred this long indifferent people to awareness, but the example of their actions (examined from this new perspective) convinces their judges of mankind's worth, if not that of these individual (and reprobate) men. In *Tunnel*, however, intrigue is cursory at best. What little there is merely serves as a positioning device: the youths are brought together and isolated from their surroundings by a constant threat of attack or enemy menace. But once in this vacuum, their society develops unhampered. Here, in fact, Heinlein treats the pattern of intrigue with open irony. He gives a twist to our expectations by undercutting the idea of denouement itself. Warned of hostile "stobor," the youths think themselves threatened, and immediately assume that their aggressor must be "human." They build elaborate fortifications around their colony, only to discover that the real enemy is within. Only in the end do they learn their error—the planet is uninhabited in the way they thought. In true serendipitous manner, however, this wrong is right after all. The environment holds other dangers than scheming men: their ramparts do serve, but to divert a seasonal migration, and to protect against a previously tame animal driven wild. These heroes "save" no one in the anticipated manner—neither the human race, nor even themselves. One fine day the time gate opens again—its closure was an accident, and this is rectified at last. The marooned students are to be fetched back to Earth. The ultimate twist is that they do not even want to be rescued. For the most hardy of these pioneers, this is home. In the end (as we have come to expect), a new core is formed within an already elite group. It results, though, in reverse fashion, not from action or even movement, but from resistance to these.

Although these books are interesting examples, the high points of action and intrigue in Heinlein's work are *Rocket Ship Galileo* and *The Puppet Masters*. Heinlein is often praised for the quality of his intrigue. It is these two works that we can best measure the extent to which intrigue leads an independent existence in his fiction. We will find it, even here, oddly qualified, mitigated by the need to shape parables. Billed as "the classic Moon flight novel that inspired modern astronautics," *Galileo* remains a narrative very much in the tradition of the pulp serial. Brassy chapter headings like "Let the Rockets Roar," and melodramatic cliff hangers like "Danger in the Desert" betray its origins. As is typical of certain pulp adventures, flamboyant scenes of action alternate with fictionalized lectures to young scientists. Here, in a chapter like "The Method of Science," school is in session. This scarcely dramatized scene imparts an ideal as well as information—the older scientist of genius questions his three junior charges on the essentials of method. They learn while working in this most perfect of educational situations. But the doing remains primary here; such scenes are never more than interludes in the action. They may be handy as fillers sometimes—for example, what better thing to do during free-fall than conduct class? Such digressions, however, are always controlled in this novel by the exigencies of intrigue. Once the action starts on the Moon, there is no time for school. Things are just the opposite in an earlier narrative like "Beyond this Horizon" (1942). Here, the characters hardly find time to act. The few episodes of intrigue seem added merely to enliven the series of dialogues that expose the central problem of genetic engineering. These, rather than the feeble actions of the Order of the Wolf, dominate and impel this story. In *Galileo*, there is hardly enough time to explore the city of the original lunar dwellers. The heroes are too busy with the Nazis; and though the Nazis used these ancient tunnels as a base, they neither noticed nor cared where they were. In the compass of this novel, the mystery is hardly touched: the heroes bring back some pictures, and the Moon dwellers remain in limbo. In later novels, however, similar mysteries suddenly expand to overwhelm the initial conflict. As early as *Red Planet*, the enigmatic Martians awake, and Heinlein's subplot suddenly suspends and invalidates the intrigue.

The two strands of *Galileo*—the scientific epic of the Moon voyage and the espionage plot—are skillfully interwoven at the outset of the tale. Three small-town junior scientists experiment with a "Moon-rocket," and it blows up. A man is found knocked out on the ground nearby. They fear a lawsuit, only to discover that the man is one of the boys' uncles, a famous scientist, Dr. Donald Cargraves. Cargraves is uninjured by the explosion. Spies are dogging his path, harassing him and committing acts of sabotage; we will not learn who exactly they are until the end. Cargraves has the knowledge to build a rocket, but he needs help to do so. Like Pinero, this maverick finds no one in the establishment to support him. He turns to these three eager American boys, and they accept. As the story advances, the emphasis is less on how the ship is built than on how native ingenuity gets around the various problems that arise. *Galileo* celebrates this aspect of the American mind. Only the evocation of the frontier spirit can pry these minors away from their parents, giving them the liberty to explore the heavens. To celebrate it full, however, a foil is needed. What better one in 1947 than Nazis on the Moon?

As the narrative progresses, the interrelation of these two lines becomes more awkward. On the ship's construction site in the deserts of New Mexico, a saboteur's bomb explodes—the ship is damaged, and Ross is blinded. All this is anticlimatic, however: the boy's sight returns miraculously, the vessel is patched up without the least difficulty. Again, just as they are about to take off, a restraining order appears. But the officers of the law are too easily persuaded to ignore it: they fall for a lame bit of Heinleinian casuistry (we're on Federal land, this is a state order). When were police ever so tractable? It is as if destiny were guiding our heroes. On the Moon, in fact, they encounter much greater danger. The *Galileo* is bombed by ruse—they expect to find no one there, let alone an enemy. But some providence saves them here as well. As elsewhere in Heinlein, men must physically inhabit a piece of ground in order to claim it. Obeying this basic instinct (which seems to be the birthright of Heinlein's elect), they build a shelter away from the ship, and the equipment is saved. In rapid sequence, they overpower the enemy ship, and bomb their base. Again, what luck! They hit when everyone is sleeping; all are killed except the leader, Major von Hartwick. This, however, turns out to be fortunate too, for our heroes have a problem on their hands: they have the German ship, but don't know how to operate it. Intrigue and action have lost their shaping role here. What we get instead is a series of illustrative happenings, each one a revelation of the marvelous ways of destiny. Significantly, *Galileo* ends not with a battle but with a trial. This scene, however, is anything but a trial in the sense of impartial judgment. Its purpose is to force the secrets of the German ship out of von Hartwick. This is done not by clever forensics, or even by superior ruse: Cargraves simply threatens to push him out on the airless planet. In a deeper sense, these proceedings are simply an excuse to vituperate the "master race," and to expose its spokesman ("von Nitwit") as a fool and groveling coward. In the Nazis, we find Heinlein's old enemy, the mindless network of ciphers. Against it, our American heroes represent that ideal union of free men operating under a canopy of unquestioned law and discipline. The outcome of this confrontation, as the story progresses, is less and less in doubt—it is a battle of devils and angels.

Behind the intrigue of *Galileo*, we recognize the familiar allegory of election.

These three boys of mixed extraction (Jenkins, Abrams, Mueller) are average small-town American scientists. Their faith in Moon travel predisposes them perhaps to their fate. But what of all the others, in towns across the country, apparently just as faithful and worthy? All serve who sit and wait, but these three are chosen, inexplicably. They have no special merit or achievements. In fact, their elevation begins paradoxically with failure: their wrong rocket ship (the product of their unaided efforts) must blow up so that the right one can carry them to the Moon and glory. The arrival of Cargraves, the actions of the Nazis, are all part of some greater plan. In spite of this substratum, however, intrigue remains a potent developing force in *Galileo*. First and foremost, it is the linear thrust of this anti-Nazi plot, and not some abstract process of grace, that pulls this group of heroes together. Serendipity there is, but it is given a local habitation and name. The trial at the end may be moot. But here, at least, the heroes themselves conduct it, and not (as in *Red Planet*) some vertically intrusive higher power. And a Nazi stands accused, not mankind itself.

The narrative pattern on which *The Puppet Masters* is built is also a variation on the tale of spy intrigue. Will-destroying parasites invade an America of the future in flying saucers. A secret police (of which the hero-narrator is part) is given the mission to stop them. This promising start gives way to sinuous advance. Gradually, allegory undermines the initial focus on action, and the strongly Calvinist implications of the theme unfold. Several parallel lines of development appear. Beyond the struggle between man and his alien enemy lies a situation that pits men against men: how to tell who is "possessed," and who is not. This in turn prefigures another, more central division, for man possessed is man fallen. On one plane, Heinlein is committed to a line of action— save these "hagridden" men. On another plane, however, his concern is quite different: to discover the infected ones and isolate them, and by doing so bring to light an inner circle of men who cannot be possessed. Against this false process of election, which yields mindless masters and slaves, Heinlein places the true force of grace. Ultimately, his chosen ones do not save themselves through their deeds, rather they are saved, carried forward by some higher plan, of which the "slugs" themselves are part. Once this is revealed, the heroes go on to rescue mankind. But they do not redeem him. They abandon him instead; their own newly-discovered destiny is apart and elsewhere.

Masters sets two secret groups against each other. Within human society, the "slugs" create a society of zombies—they leave the outer form, but take their victims' wills. At one point, the "Old Man," head of the secret police, is accused of doing the same. He makes the difference clear: "The most I ever do is to lead a man on the path he wants to follow." This Old Man is described again and again as having a "Satanic grin." His counterpart in the animal kingdom is the cantankerous ape "Old Satan." Obviously, the will to say no against odds, and to stand up to the consequences, is associated with the arch rebel of Romantic literature. The "slugs" offer man just the opposite—utopian bliss beyond striving, "nirvana." In this novel, the Romantic theme of tyranny through system, an enslavement through dull beatitude, is alive. Heinlein easily incorporates it into the dynamic of his secularized Calvinism. The real directing force is not such petty pretenders at deity as the "slugs," but the predestined plan hidden to all but the chosen few. Actually, we find here the same conflict, and the same sort of "enemy," as in *Galileo*. Only the frame is more sophisticated.

In *Masters*, the function of the tyrannical god in the Romantic system is given to parasites of the most physically repulsive sort. They come (we learn) from Titan, the sixth satellite of Saturn. Ironically, they are called "titans," with a small "t." These giants are fallen, and visibly bear the marks. They operate among men of three sorts. At the extremes, there are the "renegades"—men so depraved they need not be possessed, but serve the enemy of their own free will—and the heroes. These latter—the narrator, the Old Man and Mary—form a Heinleinian nuclear family by blood and election. Some miraculous destiny, apparently, keeps them from being possessed or depraved. In between, there are the vast majority of men. The struggle is the one we have seen before—this great pool of humanity must be free, kept open to the unforeseeable movements of election. "Possession" here is a form of damnation. Human actions do not cause it—the victims have done nothing to incur wrath or merit punishment—nor can they save themselves from it. Those ridden by the "masters" experience the "ache of guilt and despair." Their fallen state is visible through actual physical deformity—the riders give them a humped back, and their human steeds soon regress to a state of animal filth and indolence. The nature of this menace leads to some curiously Puritanical stripping games. First, "Schedule Bare Back," and then "Schedule Sun Tan" are declared. Instead of clothes mercifully concealing the prints of original sin, in this situation they hinder its fearless exposition. All are forced to peel, to reveal their true nature. Not to strip is to be shot; but to bear the mark of the slug is to die as well. There is more than a little of the Last Judgment here.

To overcome this enemy takes more than unaided human effort. Salvation demands the concurrence of a higher plan—and it is this drama that gradually usurps the role of the initial intrigue. The hero is taken by the slugs, only to be mysteriously reclaimed by the Old Man. It is never explained how the latter finds him; nor do we understand why the hero, lightning-fast on the draw elsewhere, is unable to perform here, as if the very presence of the Boss overawes him. All three members of this inner circle, in fact, undergo this same ritual of possession and exorcism. Invariably, one of the others is close by; salvation, however, is less the result of individual actions than of some act of God. Late in the novel (anticlimactically so), the Old Man himself is captured by the one surviving slug. He holds the hero prisoner and attempts to fly away to Yucatan. *In extremis*, the latter smashes the parasite, but the plane plummets earthward out of control. Miraculously, they are saved—they are over water at the time.

The slugs are dominated not by man in general, but by special men—this inner group of elect. They cannot be defeated in open battle—this would decimate the hosts as well. The real place of contention is bounded by one man's mind. The hero must submit to the parasite's control a second time, so that it in turn can be controlled. This scene resembles an exorcism more than anything else. The Old Man interrogates the slug through its host: the battle of wills takes place in the mind of the hero. Nor is this completely a conscious act of valor on the latter's part. Not only must he be tied down during the cross-examination; he must be pushed into doing it as well. The slug is, significantly, his old "master," and he fears it. He fears even more for Mary when he sees that she is to take his place. Later, he blames her for tricking him; and if she did not, then the Old Man (who engineered the whole thing) did. Actually, however, the real manipulator is the hand of destiny itself. The slugs are sterile creatures. They reproduce by "fission" (much later, when Lazarus Long clones another being from himself, he must consecrate its individuality by physically making love to it). Their linkage with hosts is fruitless: men ignore hygiene, begin to die of plagues—these "masters" are not even fit to hold slaves. Here, however, in union with the hero, a creative contact is established. This time it is man who possesses the slug. In spite of his resistance, the enemy reveals his home planet. This drawing forth is less a consequence of the Old Man's persuasive actions than of some inexplicable current of grace functioning on the unconscious or racial level of the hero's mind. The Old Man merely ticks off the names of the planets, and the link fuses: "when he came to the right one, I knew."

Moreover, just as there are two types of "masters" here, there is a wrong and a right way of possessing the mind: one way closes off the channels of grace, the other opens them. The struggle against this enemy (it turns out) will not be decided in the various "schedules" or aggressive campaigns—these invariably fail—but once again in the memory of one member of the inner circle, Mary. In several respects she is a special person. As a child, she was a member of the small colony of "Whitmanites," apostles of self-reliance. When this group is overcome by the slugs, then decimated by a fatal Venusian fever, she manages to survive both. This was an act of God; by reproducing it, the elite circle of men can destroy the parasites. Infected with this disease, they will die before their hosts. Men can be immunized and hopefully saved. But what fever did Mary have? The scientists probe the deepest recesses of her mind by all the means available to them. The hero objects to their methods—she must participate consciously in the process: "Damn it . . . those records were snitched out of my wife's head and they belong to *her*. I'm sick of you people trying to play God. I don't like it in a slug and I don't like it any better in a human being. She'll make up her own mind." Only certain people can play God, it seems. The concerted efforts of these scientists fail until, suddenly, the answer comes to her unbidden—she had "nine day fever." Things are so simple ("why didn't you ask me?") and yet inexplicable. She was not supposed to have any memories whatsoever of that period: how could she know? With this revelation, the whole design becomes clear. The saving sickness itself is nicely calibrated in terms of time. Heaven and Earth were created in seven days,

48

the slugs die in two, leaving seven days to reclaim the possessed carriers. In the same vein, it is the very nature of the enemy which will bring about its destruction in the end. Because it is "a single organism availing itself of more space," one germ can kill it all—its mode of reproduction becomes its mode of annihilation. The beautiful symmetry of this plan is revealed in a sudden burst of light. The incredible chain of events that leads up to it evolves parallel to the spy plot. All at once, at this point of crossover, we see the acts of conventional heroism that went before as insignificant and futile.

Masters has the fast beginning of the classic tale of intrigue. The narrator-hero seems familiar as well: we have the hard-boiled pragmatist-he is a doer, not a thinker. In his crisp, epigramatic mode of speech we sense a world view that is rigid and tightly compartmented.

Moreover, he is clearly a subordinate, a man who has never questioned his position in the hierarchy. He rushes into action, and throughout is never led to doubt or grow. The man does not change, but his status does: again the process of evolution is set just beyond the effect of individual deeds or blunders. Halfway through the story, there is an apparently gratuitous revelation—the Old Man really is the hero's old man, his flesh and blood father. Does this explain his sudden rise to prominence in the end, when he overleaps the normal chain of command to become "Boss" himself? Less than an act of will, ascendency here is more an access of grace. The confrontation over Mary is actually a metamorphosis—out of it emerges a "new man." this change, however, was determined in the seed, predestined both in terms of blood and those Heinleinian patterns of election that guide mankind on his expansionist quest. In this novel, as in *Galileo*, intrigue continues to the end: from time to time, the hero goes out on a mission, and the final operation, "Schedule Fever," is carried out to save mankind. These are perfunctory, however. They have become, in fact, a mask for the much different drama of grace. The fate of the survivors and a planet in ruins are lost in the exaltation of the new campaign the chosen few will carry to Titan: "Puppet Masters—the free men are coming to kill you!"

A HEINLEIN MASTERPIECE

The other major shaping pattern in Heinlein's novels of adventure (a pattern present in most of his fiction to some degree) is that of initiation. Several kinds of initiatory experience must be distinguished here: First, there is the novel of *Bildung*—the individual is mysteriously chosen for admission in some select group, and actively guided by its members through a series of trials to the goal. These works are the most backward-looking; often, they seem little more than elaborate extensions of a novella like "Gulf." Then there is the novel of false heroic formation—individual deeds and accomplishments turn out, in the end, to be superfluous: all along the hero has been following the guiding hand, intimate and invisible, of grace. In this overleaping election, the heroic conventions are subverted. Finally, there is *Have Space Suit, Will Travel.* This seems an unusual novel for Heinlein, for not only is the hero a free agent to an appreciable degree, but his individual acts have a real bearing on the outcome of events. Has the author simply relaxed his stance, and fallen back upon the stock juvenile formula? On the contrary, *Space Suit* is very much Heinlein, very much concerned with election and the destiny of the human race. A marvelous dynamic balance has been struck here between two states—heroic insecurity and sureness of the elect—which elsewhere function as contraries. In spite of its infelicitous title, this novel is a masterpiece.

Heinlein's period of juvenile adventure is roughly bracketed by two works that bear much resemblance to each other—*Space Cadet* (1948) and *Starship Troopers* (1959). Both represent a crude variation on the novel of *Bildung* as Goethe practiced it. In Goethe's work, coming of age is seen as a process which prepares the individual to assume his social responsibilities. To this worthy (and classic) goal, some modern factors are added. The hero (as the name Wilhelm Meister implies) is both everyman and a special man. Or rather, the "master" is somehow immanent in the bumbling commoner, and only waits to be drawn out. Mysteriously, he is chosen to become part of a powerful secret society, and guided until he discovers his true vocation. The hero is separated from the ordinary world; the society to which he accedes is an elite within the general society of man—benevolent, aristocratic, above the law. *Space Cadet* is exactly this kind of tale. Here, the dream of the inner circle is incarnate in an even more romantic vision of the military organization. The bulk of this story focuses on the apparatus that trains the hero. Individual action is relegated to a brief coda, in which Matt Dodson (now aware of his role in this elite group) performs a mission. The heroic act is illustrative rather than formative.

In a later novel, *Starman Jones* (1953), we have a significantly different process of initiation. Not only is the shaping group gone, but the hero finds himself apparently thrown against a select clique which stands for repression rather than election. In this future world, choice jobs in an overcrowded society are controlled by hereditary guilds. A country boy, Max Jones, dreams of becoming an astrogator, but his ambitions are thwarted by the guild. He ships out under false papers, and, finally, through a series of accidents and crises on board, comes to prove his ability. Like Andy Libby in "Misfit," Jones also possesses latent mathematical genius. He saves the ship, and in the end gets his job. Growing up, it seems, is a much different process here: this boy appears to shape his own future through acts of perseverance and courage. But does he really do so? Traditionally, heroes are superior men. But if they differ from us, it is more in degree than in kind: the possess a greater force of will, or a higher capacity for suffering, or more willingness to risk their existence in perilous actions. If we look twice, we suddenly see that Jones is not such a hero at all. Far from smashing the caste system, his acts only serve to confirm its validity by revealing that he (by inalienable right) belongs among their number. Max's Uncle, after all, was a member of the guild—his nephew is denied entrance by a legal technicality. The action in this novel becomes an elaborate process of sifting and purifying—such artificial barriers must be swept away. Max's innate mathematical abilities, in the first place, are tangible proof of the reality of this hereditary system. Significantly, these are accompanied by a memory which is quite "racial" in nature. Though the guild unjustly takes the astrogator's tables from him, Max preserves them in his brain. And so, when the ship is lost, and all seems hopeless, Max can step in and save the day. In this story, men have usurped positions rightfully belonging to the elect. Under the "natural" pressure of events, the false and weak fall away, succumbing to senility or paranoia. As ever in Heinlein's universe, the attempts of the non-elect to rule are only self-damning. In *Starman Jones*, Heinlein offers the promise of heroic adventure and of growth in action, and then cancels them out in a flash.

In both cases, Heinlein forces us to read the adventure of initiation allegorically. On one hand, the process of *Bildung*, is made to incarnate an older, more familiar form of "common grace." On the other, the classic adventure story is overturned by the revelation that its "free" hero has been following a preordained path all along. Here things turn in a different direction. In the surprising career of Max Jones, there is perhaps the analogue of that other direct and overleaping mode of grace. In a later novel like *Stranger in a Strange Land*, Heinlein strikes a new balance between the elect group and the individual recipient of "supernatural" grace. Here is a new centrifugal form in which grace, as an expanding center, comes to dominate the structural rhythms of the whole. Heinlein has also given us another alternative to this dichotomy. The one tale of initiation that escapes this easy conversion into allegory is *Have Space Suit, Will Travel* (1958). The last of the Scribner juveniles, it looks across the gulf of a year at Heinlein's next effort in the vein—*Starship Troopers*. It is hard to imagine two more disparate treatments of the same theme—the coming of age. *Space Suit* remains a tale of election and destiny. Its patterns are relaxed, while those of *Troopers* are harsh and rigid. This time, within the broader frame, there is latitude for individual action. True, the story has a typical Heinleinian confrontation: a young boy stands at the bar of universal justice, and is called upon to defend the human race against the charges of these superior aliens, to thwart the menace of punishment—man's extermination. Again, the center makes direct contact with the circumference. Rather than elision, this time there is unbroken linear development from one extreme to the other: the adventure pattern holds. Symbol and concrete object relate to each other in a manner resembling causality. If Kip's actions are exemplary, it is not at the expense of his personal drama of formation, but because of it. As we shall see, in fact, he would never have evolved as a chosen representative of the human race had he not also grown as an individual. Election is only the starting point, and destiny the end. If the path here seems too full of twists and fortunate surprises, these are interlinked each step of the way with real, believable human agents. The plan works in *Space Suit*, but it is not so absolute or restrictive. The elect are less obvious, less certain. Mankind is not so rigidly divided, nor are human will, heroic deeds, always blatantly superfluous. In its more tentative nature *Have Space Suit—Will Travel* is interesting Heinlein. Somehow in this novel, the contrary patterns of heroic adventure and predestination reach a moment of miraculous balance.

In *Space Suit*, Heinlein achieves the conflation of personal adventure and exemplum through skillful use of the first person narrator. As we watch the story develop through Kip's eyes, we believe, as he does, that his adversaries are the "Wormfaces," some monstrous alien race, the obvious villain of the classic space opera. A shock comes when he realizes that his true enemies are those he thought his friends. As if this were not enough, there is a counter-shock. Through more startling revelations, Kip finally understands that it is not a matter of friends and enemies at all, but of man's place in the universe, of his validity as a race. This exemplary situation, where a young American dreamer and his battered space suit come to stand for humanity as a whole, is not the product of ellipsis. It results instead from a clearly triadic rhythm—thesis, antithesis, synthesis—in which the logical action of the hero's mind becomes inseparable from the progression of events. This is contained within the familiar undulatory frame of point and circumference—Kip goes from his small, Midwestern town to the intergalactic court and back again. But there is a middle here also, and unbroken movement forward. Less, perhaps, than any other Heinlein adventure, *Space Suit* is not engulfed in an amorphous center, where hordes of teachers prepare their neophyte for his coming ordeals. Whatever pause there is in *Space Suit* remains no more than a lull before the storm. All at once, the mentor turns into a potential executoner, and Kip and his friend Peewee are hurled into a situation beyond all previous understanding. The twist here (and it is a fortunate one) is that they have not been groomed. On the contrary, they are thrown back upon their naked humanity. The two children defend their race as any man might do, by displaying both its strengths and weaknesses. Ironically, it is this (and only this) that saves them, and all mankind with them.

The climactic scene of *Space Suit* is a trial of cosmic proportions: in fact, man is only one of several "questionable" races to be judged. The courtroom is a favorite Heinlein locale. But his trials are usually moot affairs; they serve (as in *The Star Beast*) to display witty forensics while the reader looks on and cheers, or to showcase the talents and ideas of various superheroes, from Pinero to Jubal Harshaw. Here, however, in the workings of these fabulous proceedings, there is real suspense. As mutually valid arguments clash and contend, the action advances implacably, and we find ourselves holding our collective breath. First the "Wormfaces," from whose clutches Kip and Peewee rescued the "Mother Thing," are judged and condemned, their entire race being "rotated," thrown into some alternate dimension. The adolescents look on, and applaud this act of justice. But then, to their great surprise, they themselves are summoned before the bar. The "Mother Thing," it turns out, is a galactic policewoman. Duty demands that she bring these creatures who saved her life to trial, and she must comply. After rescuing this alien, the children spend an Elysian interlude on her planet in the Vegan system: their rooms on Earth and all their belongings are exactly reproduced for them. This ultimate courtesy is actually a scientific experiment. Through them, their race is investigated and studied. The resulting data prompts the decision to try mankind. In the eyes of his accusers, it seems, man's brutality and violence (Kip had given the Vegan "historian" his views of humanity's bloody past) make him intrinsically as undesirable as the "Wormfaces." And his intelligence makes him far more dangerous.

Kip's world is literally turned upside down. He and Peewee expect praise for their heroic deeds; instead, they become prime exhibits before the dock. Over this situation the shadow of Calvinism once again seems to hover. Their deeds prove meaningless. Because of them, in fact, man shows himself all the more a fallen creature. They would appear to have no recourse. Beside them stand two other specimens of the human race, gleaned at random throughout time—a Neanderthal and a Roman centurion. These two reply with animal fury, and are denounced beyond recall as examples of man's fundamental savagery. The cause seems lost. Then the two children (as more advanced specimens on the evolutionary scale) are called to the stand, and Kip is asked to make a statement in man's defense. But words apparently have no more impact than actions. Kip's answer is a familiar one: a fighting spirit is essential for any intelligent race if it is to survive and go forward. The boy's defense is all the more moving in its spontaneity. He has not been schooled in abstract principles; nor does he miraculously find his own humble ideas in accord with the teachings of some great authority, as is the case with Larry Smythe and the legendary Bonforte in *Double Star*. He is simply angry. As Kip champions the right of individual man to grow and develop freely as best he can, an idea naturally becomes flesh. The judges he defies hold the opposite view of things: they demand the social contract; limits and restraints must always be placed on wild growth. Their demand is reasonable, and man (as these specimens have proven) is apparently intractable to it. Does he not deserve to be destroyed? At this point, we see another twist which has more than a taint of Calvinism. If mankind is fallen, its accusers turn out to be even more so. The ensuing dialectic seriously qualifies their "superior" position, and thus rejects the idea of a rationally predictable evolution on the universal scale in favor of a more selective (and only apparently erratic) advancement by grace. In *Space Suit*, this latter force is seen both in collective terms—Kip himself condemns the Neanderthal as hopeless, but admires the courage of the equally barbarious centurion—and in its individual form. The hero is not just any boy, picked up at random or by accident. There is a predisposition—he is a special boy with special mental attitudes. And there is a predetermined plan—in the end we see that Kip, however "unsuited" he may have seemed, was the right choice after all.

The philosophy of Kip's judges is the product of their physical existence: "I am partly machine, which part can be repaired, replaced, recopied; I am partly alive, these parts die and are replaced. My living parts are more than a dozen dozens of dozens of civilized beings from throughout three Galaxies, any dozen dozens of which may join my non-living part to act." This is a collective existence very much like that of the Little People in *Methusaleh's Children* (1941). They, however, were a corporation of wholly living parts; here, organic and inorganic components alike have become replaceable and inter-changeable. It is surely ironic that such an entity uses the first person singular pronoun. Throughout his career, Heinlein's attitude toward these non-indivi-dual modes of eternal life is clear. In his most recent novel, *Time Enough for Love*, the computer "Minerva" gives up eternity as a machine to become a free (but relatively mortal) being of flesh and blood. The same Lazarus Long who applauds her decision had recoiled in horror at the Little People. These composite beings are the arch-enemies of Heinlein's man. They are formidable because their vision of things is so tempting: is it not a rational solution to the human condition? The answer for Heinlein is always a resounding *"no!"* Such "reason" is alien to man's basic individuality. If there is to be immortal-ity, it must perpetuate the concrete and unique body of man himself. The pro-cess which brings certain men to seek this is profoundly elective in nature. In *Space Suit*, however, this Heinleinian vision is neither asserted or preached. Instead, it evolves subtly and forcefully from the dramatic encounter of two very ephemeral children with an adversary whose strengths and weaknesses are thoroughly rooted in his own corporeal existence.

The dialectic of *Space Suit* shows just how strongly Heinlein's vision goes against the philosophy of the Enlightenment, and hence that mode of scientifc "progress" with which he is often associated. These judges view the universe impersonally and statistically. To them, men have no individuality; thus, any "sampling" will explain man's nature: "They [men] are not independent individuals; they are parts of a single organism. Each cell in your body con-tains your whole pattern. From three samples of the organism you call the human race I can predict the future potentialities and limits of that race." Herein lies the obvious ludicrousness of their choice of "specimens." Their procedure is as foolish as any form of xenophobia in Heinlein, but far more sub-tle, for its justification is the scientific method itself. In many Heinlein works, the hero fights his way clear of just such logical rigidity, replacing double-valued thinking with the freedom of a multi-valued mode. He attacks, in the same way, all arbitrary restrictions: there must be a floating pool of free individuals, just as there must be unlimited doors by which to escape from the logical traps and prisons of the mind. Yet, paradoxically, this freedom exists only so that the "right" people or ideas may be chosen. All polyvalence in Heinlein is ultimately (and inexorably) reduced to his fundamental bipolarity—that rhythm of election and destiny which replaces whatever arbitrary boundaries man in his enlight-ened ignorance draws around himself. Thus, the judges' organic analogy is faulty: in the individual body, each cell may contain the whole pattern, but each man does not contain the whole race. This cannot be true if there is to be election. And yet, to have as many patterns as there are people is equally ab-horrent. Heinleinian genetics are much simpler: there are "star lines," and then the others—the chosen and the reprobate. The strength of *Space Suit* is that it acts out in dramatic terms what elsewhere is often simply asserted. These judges, in their scientific "objectivity," back themselves into a corner. They fail to understand the apparently erratic, illogical, subjective reactions of two human children. Faced with this mystery, they are ironically obliged to grant them more time, if only (like the Martians in *Stranger in a Strange Land*) to continue their observations of this peculiarly complex race.

In response to the judges' indictment against humanity, Kip blurts out defiantly: "We have no limits! There's no telling what our future will be." In refusing to be governed, he refuses determinism as well. Is this not also a rejection of the higher governance of predestination? One of the unusual things about Heinlein's universe is that it unfolds according to a plan which is both predestined and open-ended. Indeed, Heinlein's heroes will probe limits only to refuse them. In fact, each time a new door is opened, or a new dimension entered, a closed system is invariably created, like Waldo's perpetual motion energy machine. The real relation between individual man and cosmos is vertical: here or anywhere, by an act of election, the polar dynamic can arise. In this way, Heinlein as future historian denies all historical or eschatological dimension to his world. Implicit in the very idea of this trial and judgment in *Space Suit* is a historical vision. And yet this is as wrong as the judges' process of "scientific" selection. If Kip is brought to the bar, and if his coming is ultimately fortunate, some other pattern chooses him. Surprisingly, this unlikely boy becomes the savior of mankind. The frame at least is vertical. But within it there is no ellipsis: surprise this time if suspense. Once again, the movement from pole to pole is not a leap, but an unbroken dialectical advance.

The judges respond to Kip's outburst: "It may be true that you have no limits. . . that is to be determined. But, if true, it is not a point in your favor. For we have limits." We seem to have stalemate. At this point, however, a subtle imbalance is created that will tip the action in new, unexpected directions. The judges are not as rational as they would seem. An undercurrent of anxiety runs through their speech as they contemplate these feeble and helpless humans before them: "They [men] have no art and only the most primitive of science, yet such is their violent nature that even with so little knowledge they are now energetically using it to exterminate each other. Their driving will is such that they may succeed. But if by some unlucky chance they fail, they will inevitably, in time, reach other stars. It is this possibility which must be calculated: how soon they will reach us, if they live, and what their potentialities will be then." This is nothing but the old familiar vision of "serendipity," presented from the opposite side. The judges' irrational fears burst through the statistical jargon. In seeking to condemn man, they praise him. In this light, we listen to Kip's awkward, impassioned, and apparently futile defense of art and culture on Earth with awakened interest. Perhaps man has some value after all; perhaps his cause is not as lost as it seems.

The conflict between man the individualist and collective forces or repressive institutions is far more interestingly developed in *Space Suit* than elsewhere in Heinlein. On the other extreme stands a book like *Farnham's Freehold* (1964). Here the cards are stacked in a particularly repugnant way. Displaced in time by an atomic explosion, Hugh Farnham and his entourage are hurled into a future society ruled by Blacks. This novel reads like a racist's nightmare: white men are now bound up in hereditary slavery; the only way to advance is to submit to castration. The Black rulers are either decadent, cruel, or both. The climax of this narrative is also a courtroom scene. Hugh Farnham screams defiance at this blatantly unjust system, in which man (or at least white man) has become merely an experimental animal, without the least personal freedom. Again, a tenacious individualism wins awe, if not respect. Again, an apparently suicidal outburst turns out to be more fortunate than anyone could have imagined. Because he is incomprehensible to these world-weary rulers, he is sent back to his bombed-out present. But what seems an even worse predicament turns out to be, with the help of a handy time paradox, a blessing. Hugh arrives in the old world *before* the blast that displaced him, and is able to take refuge in time. Free humanity survives the holocaust—and because of this, of course, the slave world of the future will never be. The only problem here is the suggestion that "free man" equals "white man." How can we not believe this, when we learn, with Hugh, that his Black masters, in spite of their veneer of civilization, are cannibals in the worst sense? Some of Heinlein's ecology-minded aliens practice a more beneficient form of flesh-eating, disposing of their dead on the dinner table, wasting no speck of food or energy. Farnham's Blacks, however, raise white virgins for table meat. In *Freehold*, racism is restored to an old role in a fundamentalist context. The whole Black race is reprobate. Allowed to evolve in their alternate world, they gradually destroy man's already fallen state. The most sophisticated uses of reason only lead to more terrible abuses of the human form divine. In a stroke of grace, this whole world vanishes. It never was and never will be—a bad dream at best.

No such obsession mars the complex development of *Space Suit*. Here the judges have an argument which, even in the Heinleinian context, has at least partial validity. Heinlein is not *a priori* against rules or binding customs, especially when survival is at stake. Thus, in *Time for the Stars* (1956), Uncle Steve's stern doctrine of military discipline holds Tom from mutiny, keeping the collective effort from disintegrating. Anarchy is as bad as slavery. Men may feel they are no more than "spare parts" in a space-borne laboratory; yet their subservience is justified in a sense by the fortunate results. What we have here actually is individuality (each scientist pursues his own personal interests) framed by a general purpose, and vindicated by unhoped-for success. If this is Heinlein's ideal, it is realized in dramatic rather than allegorical terms in *Space Suit*. Things at one point look grim for mankind. The Neanderthal shows himself a brute; the Centurion, violent and crafty as well, is worse. In these judges' eyes, the chain of evolution is reversed—it becomes a line of fall. Kip's arguments appear to reveal man at his most dangerous and defiant. When all appears lost, Peewee makes a last desperate point: she confronts these implacable logicians with the altruistic folly of human heroism—Kip after all did risk his life to save the alien Mother Thing. But just as the judges dismiss man's art as irrelevant, so they would ignore Kip's selfless act. And yet it is this same illogical human capacity for self-sacrifice that will, in the end, save both the children and mankind. Man is free to throw his life away as well. If the Earth is to be "rotated," Kip and Peewee ask to be sent home: they will share the common fate of mankind. To their judges, this is the acme of absurdity. How can they, with their standardized, interchangeable parts, understand a collectivity of individuals who, though they may follow their own separate ways, freely concur in the face of adversity? In Heinlein's world, he who hesitates is lost: the judges balk, and mankind is saved.

One can, if he wishes, read *Space Suit* as an allegory. Kip builds his space suit, and one day is taken up and carried to fabulous heights. How many other boys, with suits and the same dreams, in other towns, are not taken? All of Kip's subsequent actions merely prolong the momentum of this initial election. It is interesting to note as well just how inconsequential heroic deeds in the the traditional sense have become. Reversal comes not because Kip saves the Mother Thing, but because he refuses to save himself. In doing so, he renounces this false election by the judges—better the common destiny of mankind than eternity as a museum specimen of a lost race. Refusal once again is fortunate, for Kip is chosen a second time. Mankind is granted a reprieve, not a pardon. Kip and Peewee will return to Earth, and the Mother Thing will keep in touch with them to watch over man's evolution. Within the mass of humanity, there is and will be this secret circle. There is every indication, however, that inside this circle another, tighter group is being formed. Led by men of Kip's caliber, the race may go on as predicted, and conquer even the galactic rulers themselves. As in *Puppet Masters*, the false god with his tyrannical "limits" must be overthrown if the channels of grace are to remain open, and the predestined plan be fulfilled.

The strength of *Space Suit* is to leave all this muted. First and foremost, it is a novel of adventure. In the manner of the classic juvenile romance, Kip and Peewee return to the daily routine of their former lives on Earth (perhaps a friendship has been kindled, but that is all). As they walk among men, they bear no visible signs of their election, can tell no tale of their incredible undertaking. Who would believe them? The secret must remain locked forever in their hearts. In contrast, *Farnham's Freehold* ends with ostentation. Here the inner group has become, physically, an island of light in the midst of atomic ruin. They openly display their superiority: "High above their sign their home-made starry flag is flying—and they are still going on." *Space Suit* also ends on a note of defiance. But instead of an emblem, we have more action, on a level that is both human and humorous. Back behind the counter at the soda-fountain, Kip flings a pie in the face of his small-town detractor.

AFTERTHOUGHTS

The truly "classic" Heinlein is the allegorical writer who emerges from the numerous stories and novels I have examined. There is a basic pattern, shaped in the earliest tales, and carefully elaborated in his subsequent work. But there is also a distinct development of allegorical forms on a diachronic axis as well.

The early stories and novellas are more obviously parables, and whatever action and adventure there is has an overtly symbolic or illustrative function. The middle novels are different: here, an allegorical purpose gradually informs and transforms conventional adventure. Rightfully, then, Heinlein's later "problem" novels are hybrids. In their didactic and "philosophical" emphasis, they mark a return to the more static patterns of the early stories. At the same time, however, their form has benefited from the development of Heinlein's art during the decade of juvenile writing. The curious subversion of the linear patterns of intrigue and initiation in these works has contributed as much to the form of *Stranger* as the vertical configurations of a story like "Waldo."

In spite of this merger, these adventure forms have a certain life of their own in Heinlein. Running parallel to the revival of openly philosophical works on a grand scale in the 1960s is a current of shorter works in which the impetus of a decade of action and intrigue is sustained. Though the subtitle of *Podkayne of Mars: Her Life and Times* (1963) shows that it has been touched by some new interest in exemplary fiction, the novel remains basically a juvenile adventure. *Farnham's Freehold* is essentially a tale of adventure; this time, the motive force is time instead of space travel—a "tunnel in the sky" of a different sort. *The Moon Is a Harsh Mistress* (1965) is a story of political intrigue and revolution in the manner of *Double Star*. True, these novels eventually blend with the philosophical stream, if only through the fact that their heroes get progressively older. We go in the span of a decade from youth to middle age, and finally to senescence. In Heinlein's latest work, *Time Enough for Love*, adventure of all sorts (intrigue as well as the drama of coming of age) is absorbed into a new narrative center—the exemplary life of ancient and deathless Lazarus Long.

One novel of the 1960s does stand out—*Glory Road* (1963). This last of Heinlein's juvenile adventures is an interesting work, both from its position in this decade, and in itself. It has many of the faults of the Heinlein novel in general, and a dogmatic edge that places it unquestionably in his late period. Yet somehow it remains a satisfying piece of work. Again, in a novel apparently about the formation of a hero, there is no individual growth. We have an up-to-date protagonist: a student draftee of the '60s. As if to mock us, however, his conclusive experiences do not take place on the battlefields of Southeast Asia, but on those of some fantasy kingdom a la Edgar Rice Burroughs. And are these experiences really conclusive? He leaves our world disaffected, only to return disenchanted. In terms of traditional patterns of initiation, the action centers here in another huge elision—the hero doesn't face his world, he circumvents it. But might it not have been (as the rival convention demands) only a dream after all? Heinlein strikes, it seems, a new note of ambiguity. In openly stressing the dream-motif, which has propelled the hero of many a romance into fabulous adventure, and brought him safely back again, Heinlein seemingly seeks to parody his own process of suppressing the middle.

In *Glory Road*, as in most Heinlein novels, the action slows in midstream as emphasis shifts from heroic deeds to the social and political complexities of this mythical kingdom. In this case, however, the shift is softened, and the initial thrust of the intrigue ultimately carried through, by Heinlein's masterful use of the first-person narrator. Oscar "Scar" Gordon springs from the lineage of the hero of *Puppet Masters*, and of Larry Smythe in *Double Star*. As a persistent voice, though, telling his story and commenting on it, he is far more engaging. True, he is brash and opiniated. And some of his epigrammatic judgments even rival in unpleasantness those of Jubal Harshaw or Lazarus Long. Yet he is rarely a boor, because he is rarely permitted to take himself seriously. In the twists and turns of the action, his vision of things is constantly undercut. What emerges from this clever counterpoint of events and opinions is not personal growth but just the opposite. If the hero proves anything, it is his capacity to endure, to remain buoyant.

Overwhelmingly, the heroes of Heinlein's early stories are adults. His latest novels mark a complete return to this adult world and beyond. To a critic like Brian Aldiss, no maturity of understanding seems to result from this process. On the contrary these "adult" works provide a classic case of arrested development—the mature world continually cast in terms of a retentive childhood. Perhaps Heinlein is at his best when things are turned around. In *Glory Road* (as in *Space Suit*), the juvenile hero grapples with adult problems, but in some other distant world. When he returns to his own world, the growing up still waits to be done. It seems, moreover, that Scar Gordon (like Kip before him) accomplished what he did only because he remained a child. Indeed, the essence of Heinlein's philosophy in these two novels, with its refusal of limits of any kind, tyrannical or utopian, is merely the refusal of perpetual child-man to face the light of common day. There are differences, however, between *Glory Road* and its predecessor. Kip displays this buoyancy of youth in a well-defined dramatic situation—the climactic trial scene. Scar Gordon, on the other hand, proclaims it throughout. Heinlein later tried to repeat this tour-de-force of the first-person narrator in *The Moon Is a Harsh Mistress*. But once this opiniated discourse is taken from the mouth of the forever youth, it sours. The hero's voice in this later novel of revolution and adult intrigue bogs down in its own "seriousness" (not to mention the "new-Russian" newspeak it uses for conversing). With the passing of Scar Gordon, youth fades forever from Heinlein's universe.

Glory Road also shares with *Space Suit* the same creative interplay (if to a lesser degree) between Heinlein's persistant patterns of election and predestination, and those of the action genre he adopts. *Glory* is clearly another tale of election. Scar is mysteriously visited by a ravishing blonde as he basks in the sunshine of Southern France. The contact is immediate—an elective affinity. The newspaper ad he answers was (he learns) written for him and him alone. Yet in this novel, not only is the old sword and sorcery pattern revived; it is respected throughout. There is, perhaps, more rousing adventure in this work than in most Heinlein novels: we have a progressive sequence of battles leading to a gala sword fight in the grand tradition. Again, as with *Space Suit*, the meaning of this novel is to be found not in a separation of these two strands, but in their interaction. The message, however, is a different one—and a poignant sign of the alteration in Heinlein's world view that occurred during the '60s. Scar goes down the "glory road" to the heart of a universal order that would seem a Heinleinian paradise. Instead of big government, there is no government: "Even positive edicts of the Imperium were usually negative in form—thou shalt not blow up thy neighbor's planet. Blow up your own if you wish." Democracy and freedom for all? Far from it. In this universe, the ablest rule, and order is strictly maintained. Yet even in an Eldorado such as this, Scar becomes restless—without his heroic task, the hero feels "useless." An alien on the planet Center, Scar goes back to Earth, only to discover that he is alien there too. Glory is the goal of Heinlein's man. Here, between center and circumference, it can be found only on the endless road that moves back and forth. Here begins that pattern of perpetual motion from one meaningless extreme to the other which receives its ultimate incarnation in Heinlein's latest novel. Lazarus Long moves forever between what for him are the mutually cancelling terms of time and love.

Glory Road, then, both a "classic" and an anomaly in Heinlen's canon. Less overtly allegorical than most of his works, it remains nonetheless a superb parable, in which the higher workings that control man's destiny are deftly exposed to view. On the other hand, as the last of those novels of juvenile adventure in which the patterns of action not only co-exist but actually interact with those of election, it represents in Heinlein's fiction the current that lost.

*   *   *

Dr. Slusser discusses Heinlein's latest novels in his controversial study, *Robert A. Heinlein: Stranger in His Own Land, Second Edition*, available from The Borgo Press for $1.95 per copy.

BIOGRAPHY AND BIBLIOGRAPHY

ROBERT ANSON HEINLEIN was born July 7, 1907, at Butler, Missouri, the son of Rex Ivar and Bam (Lyle) Heinlein. After graduating from the U.S. Naval Academy at Annapolis in 1929, he served in the Navy until receiving his discharge in the mid-1930s. His first professional story, "Life-Line," appeared in the August, 1939 issue of *Astounding Science Fiction*. Heinlein married Virginia Gerstenfeld in 1948. He is the only man ever to win four Hugo Awards for best SF novel of the year (for *Double Star*, *Starship Troopers*, *Stranger in a Strange Land*, and *The Moon Is a Harsh Mistress*). He was also the first recipient of the Nebula Grandmaster Award. His papers and correspondence have been collected by the University of California, Santa Cruz.

1. *Rocket Ship Galileo*. Charles Scribner's Sons, New York, 1947, 212p, Cloth, Novel
2. *Space Cadet*. Charles Scribner's Sons, New York, 1948, 242p, Cloth, Novel
3. *Beyond This Horizon*. Fantasy Press, Reading, 1948, 242p, Cloth, Novel.
4. *Red Planet*. Charles Scribner's Sons, New York, 1949, 211p, Cloth, Novel.
5. *Sixth Column*. Gnome Press, New York, 1949, 256p, Cloth, Novel
5A. reprinted as: *The Day After Tomorrow*. Signet, New York, 1951, 160p, Paper, Novel
6. *Waldo; and, Magic Inc*. Doubleday, Garden City, 1950, 219p, Cloth, Coll.
6A. reprinted as: *Waldo: Genius in Orbit*. Avon, New York, 1958, 191p, Paper, Coll.
7. *The Man Who Sold the Moon*. Shasta, Chicago, 1950, 288p, Cloth, Coll.
8. *Farmer in the sky*. Charles Scribner's Sons, New York, 1950, 216p, Cloth, Novel
9. *Between Planets*. Charles Scribner's Sons, New York, 1951, 222p, Cloth, Novel
10. *The Green Hills of Earth*. Shasta, Chicago, 1951, 256p, Cloth, Coll.
11. *Universe*. Dell, New York, 1951, 64p, Paper, Novella

11A. expanded as: *Orphans of the Sky*. Victor Gollancz, London, 1963, 160p, Cloth, Novel

12. *The Puppet Masters*. Doubleday, Garden City, 1951, 219p, Cloth, Novel

13. *Tomorrow, the Stars*. Doubleday, Garden City, 1952, 249p, Cloth, Anth.

14. *The Rolling Stones*. Charles Scribner's Sons, New York, 1952, 276p, Cloth, Novel

14A. reprinted as: *Space Family Stone*. Victor Gollancz, London, 1969, 267p, Cloth, Novel

15. *Starman Jones*. Charles Scribner's Sons, New York, 1953, 305p, Cloth, Novel

16. *Revolt in 2100*. Shasta, Chicago, 1953, 317p, Cloth, Coll.

17. *Assignment in Eternity*. Fantasy Press, Reading, 1953, 256p, Cloth, Coll.

17A. reprinted in abridged form as: *Lost Legacy*. Digit, London, 1960, 156p, Paper, Coll.

18. *The Star Beast*. Charles Scribner's Sons, New York, 1954, 282p, Cloth, Novel

19. *Tunnel in the Sky*. Charles Scribner's Sons, New York, 1955, 273p, Cloth, Novel

20. *Double Star*. Doubleday, Garden City, 1956, 186p, Cloth, Novel

21. *Time for the Stars*. Charles Scribner's Sons, New York, 1956, 244p, Cloth, Novel

22. *The Door into Summer*. Doubleday, Garden City, 1957, 188p, Cloth, Novel

23. *Citizen of the Galaxy*. Charles Scribner's Sons, New York, 1957, 302p, Cloth, Novel

24. *Methuselah's Children*. Gnome Press, Hicksville, 1958, 188p, Cloth, Novel

25. *Have Space Suit—Will Travel*. Charles Scribner's Sons, New York, 1958, 276p, Cloth, Novel

26. *Starship Troopers*. G. P. Putnam's Sons, New York, 1959, 309p, Cloth, Novel

27. *The Menace from Earth*. Gnome Press, Hicksville, 1959, 255p, Cloth, Coll.

28. *The Unpleasant Profession of Jonathan Hoag*. Gnome Press, Hicksville, 1959, 256p, Cloth, Coll.

28A. reprinted as: *6 x H*. Pyramid, New York, 1961, 191p, Paper, Coll.

29. *Stranger in a Strange Land*. G. P. Putnam's Sons, New York, 1961, 408p, Cloth, Novel
30. *Podkayne of Mars, Her Life and Times*. G. P. Putnam's Sons, New York, 1963, 191p, Cloth, Novel
31. *Glory Road*. G. P. Putnam's Sons, New York, 1963, 288p, Cloth, Novel
32. *Farnham's Freehold*. G. P. Putnam's Sons, New York, 1964, 315p, Cloth, Novel
33. *Three by Heinlein* (includes *The Puppet Masters*, *Waldo*, and *Magic, Inc.*). Doubleday, Garden City, 1965, 426p, Cloth, Coll.
33A. reprinted as: *A Heinlein Triad*. Victor Gollancz, London, 1966, 426p, Cloth, Coll.
34. *The Moon Is a Harsh Mistress*. G. P. Putnam's Sons, New York, 1966, 383p, Cloth, Novel
35. *A Robert Heinlein Omnibus* (includes *Beyond This Horizon*, *The Man Who Sold the Moon*, and *The Green Hills of Earth*). Sidgwick & Jackson, London, 1966, 644p, Cloth, Coll.
36. *The Worlds of Robert A. Heinlein*. Ace, New York, 1966, 189p, Paper, Coll.
37. *The Past Through Tomorrow*. G. P. Putnam's Sons, New York, 1967, 667p, Cloth, Coll.
38. *I Will Fear No Evil*. G. P. Putnam's Sons, New York, 1970, 401p, Cloth, Novel
39. *The Best of Robert Heinlein*. Sidgwick & Jackson, London, 1973, 348p, Cloth, Coll.
40. *Time Enough for Love*. G. P. Putnam's Sons, New York, 1973, 605p, Cloth, Novel